VGM Professional Careers Series

CAREERS in

SCIENCE

THOMAS EASTON

FOURTH EDITION

DISCARD

VGM Career Books

Chicago   New York   San Francisco   Lisbon   London   Madrid   Mexico City
Milan   New Delhi   San Juan   Seoul   Singapore   Sydney   Toronto

Library of Congress Cataloging-in-Publication Data

Easton, Thomas A.
    Careers in science / Thomas Easton.—4th ed.
        p.   cm.—(VGM professional careers series)
    ISBN 0-07-141156-9 (alk. paper)
    1. Science—Vocational guidance.   2. Engineering—Vocational guidance.   I. Title.
II. Series.

Q147.E27   2004
502.3—dc22   2003025809

For Joellen and Kate

1 2 3 4 5 6 7 8 9 0   DOC/DOC   3 2 1 0 9 8 7 6 5 4

ISBN 0-07-141156-9

Interior design by Robert S. Tinnon

McGraw-Hill books are available at special quantity discounts to use as premiums and sales promotions, or for use in corporate training programs. For more information, please write to the Director of Special Sales, Professional Publishing, McGraw-Hill, Two Penn Plaza, New York, NY 10121-2298. Or contact your local bookstore.

This book is printed on acid-free paper.

CONTENTS

and Electronics Engineering • Environmental Engineering •
Industrial Engineering • Materials Engineering • Mechanical
Engineering • Mining and Geological Engineering • Nuclear
Engineering • Petroleum Engineering • Engineering Technicians
and Technologists • Hot Spots • Careers on Campus •
Careers in Industry • Careers in Government • Organizations
for Engineers

FOREWORD

Successful career planning is a process that requires self-knowledge, research, experimentation, analysis, and commitment. This book will provide you with a comprehensive and helpful approach to planning a career in science by providing a framework to guide you through three critical steps. Making an informed choice and developing a plan to attain your goals will result in a career that is a journey through life filled with immense personal satisfaction.

In this book, Dr. Easton has provided an excellent framework for evaluating whether a science-related career is for you. He encourages you to consider first your personality and interests, for they have a great deal to do with which aspects of science and specific jobs are right for you. Self-knowledge is the first step in career planning.

Dr. Easton surveys many career opportunities and provides accurate, timely information on educational requirements, potential for industry growth, salary expectations, and lifestyle impact. It is truly amazing how many careers involve science, and it is especially interesting to learn about new opportunities in the growing biotechnical, bioengineering, and computer technology fields. Discovering the opportunities that best suit your interests and aptitudes is half of the second step in career planning; gaining experience to confirm your choice is the other half.

As director of the Career Services Office at Thomas College, I appreciate Dr. Easton's emphasis on gaining confidence and skill through internships and research projects. Employers are seeking candidates with both education and experience. In the field of science, it is especially important to be able to demonstrate the ability to apply what you have learned in the classroom. It's easy to say, "I'm a detail-oriented, analytical thinker able to multitask," but when a water quality test fails on your first day in the lab because you omitted a crucial step from the process—well, I think you get the point! Making that same mistake as an intern feels quite different.

This book also does an excellent job of explaining the third step in the career-planning process—making the connection from training and experience to finding a job. Dr. Easton has included helpful resources for effective career exploration and job hunting and many practical tips.

Careers in science are among the most exciting and challenging. As Dr. Easton says, "No scientist has ever truly saved the world or the human species from destruction, but many who pursue careers in science have, as a result of their labors, saved or improved lives, fed the hungry, or warmed the cold. They have identified hazards, and they have found answers. They have made discoveries that spawned industries and employed thousands or millions. They defend us all against the forces of extinction, and their dedication is that of the soldier in love with the battle. Scientists often say they are the most blessed of human beings, because they are paid for doing what they would do as a hobby if they had to." If you can find a job you truly love, then it never feels like work. This book will prepare you to do just that. Enjoy!

KAREN WAGNER
Director of Career Services
Thomas College
Waterville, Maine

PREFACE

"Career development" people think of life in terms of careers. Often, they divide life into five stages:

1. *Growth.* Until about age fourteen, children develop their understanding of the meaning and purpose of work, try new experiences, and develop their self-image.

2. *Exploration.* Between the ages of fourteen and twenty-four, people realize that they need to choose a career. They look at their interests and abilities, consider how they may tie into various occupations, choose a direction for their future, and gain appropriate education, training, and experience.

3. *Establishment.* Between the mid-twenties and middle age, people develop their professional competence with further education, training, and experience. They develop occupational status, and they advance.

4. *Maintenance.* Once they have established their professional niche, people devote their efforts to preserving their skills through practice and on-the-job training. They also begin to plan for eventual retirement.

5. *Decline.* After about age sixty-five, people reduce their commitment to work. They adjust the demands of work to their own fading energies. Gradually or suddenly, they shift their attention from their work to themselves.

This scheme was first developed by Donald E. Super in the 1950s. It is still useful, and although I am not going to talk about scientific careers in terms of the five stages, one stage does define the readers of this book. Only "explorers" will be interested in anything with a title like *Careers in Science*. The exceptions will be "establishment" and "maintenance" career counselors, whose job is to help the explorers explore.

Explorers, however, need not all be under the age of twenty-four. A recession, the failure of a business or industry, or even a change in technology can put people out of work. If these individuals cannot find the same job with another employer, they must find a different job. They may even have to go back to school.

Careers rarely follow a rigid pattern. People do—and should—continue to grow throughout their lives. Many never stop exploring. Some, as soon as they are established in one career, miss the challenge of the early stages. They grow bored or stale, and they begin to look for fresh alternatives. They shift from business to science to law to politics. They may never reach the maintenance stage at all.

Personally, I admire such job-hopping jackrabbits. They sometimes seem to have a keenness and a vitality that others lack. Perhaps they have more interests and competencies. Or perhaps they lack the consuming, absorbing interests that bind others to single careers.

Certainly, any one person begins life with a host of potential careers before him or her. Interests and abilities then determine the amount and nature of the education he or she seeks—a high school diploma, an associate of arts (A.A.) or science (A.S.) degree, a bachelor of arts (B.A.) or science (B.S.) degree, a master's (M.A. or M.S.) degree, or a doctorate (Ph.D., D.A., D.Sc., M.D., or D.O.). Each level of education leads to certain careers, although some careers will require a return to school. For example, a brand-new B.S. graduate in biochemistry can be a technician, but not a university professor. The professorship requires a doctorate. But the B.S. technician can always go back to school to gain first a master's degree and then the Ph.D.

Career options need not, of course, be defined only in terms of degrees. I recall a friend who, over thirty years ago, earned his doctorate in health physics and became a researcher with the National Institutes of Health. Later in life, he enrolled in an administrative training program to pursue a new career option, leaving research for administration. He may eventually become a campus dean or a research and development (R&D) manager.

I think also of researchers who have become teachers (and vice versa) or editors or writers or entrepreneurs. In each case, the individual has grown and broadened. However, the individual has also pursued preexisting interests. A scientist never becomes a businessperson unless he or she has cared about product development, management, or sales in the past. Each step in a person's career has its roots in the person and in previous steps.

Each step in a career leads to further steps. But each step also closes off some of the early options. For instance, after twenty years as a biologist, it is difficult to go back to school and become a geologist, a nuclear physicist, or a mathematician. The shift requires too much time, and the intellectual sponge that once was the college student has usually lost too much of its absorptive capacity.

It is thus wise to make your choice carefully at the beginning. Gain all the education you have patience, time, and money for, and gain it in a field that matches your interests and abilities as closely as possible. Do you need help? That is the purpose of this book. Its topic is the career options available in the sciences. It will discuss the difference between a job and a career. It will outline what science is and what kinds of people are scientists. It will present a few statistics on the supply of and demand for scientists. It will help you choose a field of science, describe the educational requirements, and present the possibilities in the various fields of science. Finally, it will tell you a little about how to find a job in your chosen field.

Once you have completed this book, you will have a good idea of which fields of science you are most likely to find satisfying and rewarding for years to come. You will know what kinds of jobs in those fields you might fill, where they might lead you, and what education and experience you must gain to qualify for them. You will also know what personal and financial rewards to expect. You will then be ready to take the first steps toward your career in science.

CHAPTER

1

CAREERS AND SCIENCE

We begin our discussion of careers in science with a few key questions:

- What is a job?
- What is a career?
- What is science?
- What is a scientist?

We can define science and scientists in terms of the scientific method, and we will do just that in a little while. First, however, we must consider more basic matters.

JOBS VERSUS CAREERS

A job is a set of tasks or performances by which a person earns the pay necessary to buy food, shelter, clothes, and other goods in our society. A job is defined in terms of the effort that goes into it, the results it produces, or the setting in which it is performed. The individuality of the person who does the job is irrelevant.

In contrast, the person who fills a career is essential to the definition of career. The reason is simple: during one's career, one has many jobs. Those jobs may or may not be in the same field or even for the same employer. But they are all held by the same person, and the person who fills each of those jobs has been shaped by all of his or her previous jobs—as well as by that person's other roles, such as student, trainee, family member, citizen, hobbyist, and retiree. A career is thus a history, a journey through life.

For a young person, most of the career still lies ahead. It is thus a journey planned or hoped for: an end, a goal, even an ideal. One thing it is not is a means. A job is a means, for it earns the price of survival, of necessities and luxuries. A career is something more, for it is intimately involved with one's image of one self.

To this we can add something from the common wisdom. What is a "career man" or a "career woman"? Such a person is not just putting in time to earn a paycheck, but is actively pursuing a role or place in society. This person has a sense of mission—a dedication to more than mere personal or even family survival. This person may even have a calling, a vocation.

Any career begins in school. In fact, it begins before the "careerist" has a chance to make a choice. Elementary school and junior high school build basic skills and interests. High school exposes students to various broad fields, such as chemistry, biology, physics, and history. High school thus permits a choice of overall direction: will the student prepare for college, learn a trade, or prepare for the world of business? High school also leads to the first major career decisions: Will the new high school graduate get a job immediately or go on to college? Which college will he or she go to? Which trade will he or she learn? Will the new graduate join the family business—or perhaps start a new business?

College often seems more of a starting point for a career than high school, for it is in college that students first encounter the specific fields in which they might actually work. They take courses in organic chemistry and biochemistry, genetics and microbiology, astronomy, calculus, and more. They focus on areas that mesh with their interests and abilities. They gain specific knowledge essential to work in a field. They find problems, questions, and issues to which they can dedicate their lives. They set their sights on their future status and role, and they decide whether they need still more education to reach their goals.

Eventually, during or after their schooling, most students become workers. They take a first job, a first "career position" in their field. Later they may decide to pursue further training, to accept or reject responsibility, to shift from teaching to research or business or writing, or even to shift from one field to another. Their career develops as they go from decision to decision and from position to position. In general, an individual goes from student-hood to an entry-level position of little reward, power, responsibility, or free-dom to later positions of more reward, power, responsibility, and freedom. Careers in science may peak with a deanship on campus, a department chair-manship, a college or university presidency, a senior administrative post with the government, or even the presidency of a private corporation. At less rar-efied levels, many scientific careers peak with a rank of full professor or sen-ior researcher. Many more never get that far, and still more of the thousands who work in the fields of science are neither teachers nor researchers. Instead, they are technicians of various sorts, sellers of technical equipment, textbook editors, and so on, and they climb their own hierarchies, perhaps ending as chiefs of labs, heads of sales departments, and editors in chief.

In *Entrepreneurship and the Wired Life: Work in the Wake of Careers*, Fer-nando Flores and John Gray write that people fall into two broad categories: those who are self-directed and those who are community directed. Self-directed people—including many scientific researchers—seek growth, autonomy, and freedom to be creative. Community-directed people—including many academics, such as professors and deans—are committed to the long-term well-being of the groups to which they belong. Both types of people move up a "ladder of competence" (first described by philosopher Hubert Dreyfus) as they progress through their careers (see Figure 1.1).

A great many careers are available in science. The variety is awesome, and to the young person peeking tentatively through the entry door, it may be more than a little frightening. Yet all careers in science do have one thing in common: science.

WHAT IS SCIENCE?

When most people think of science, they think of white coats, laboratories, and high-powered computers. But science is science even without such superficial trimmings. At its heart is a very simple idea: check it out. People who approach the world the way scientists do are skeptical. They are not

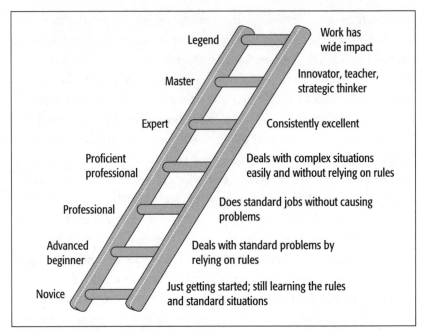

Figure 1.1 The Ladder of Competence

content to take someone else's word that anything is so, no matter how eminent an authority that someone may be. Scientific knowledge is based not on hearsay, but on reality. Scientists take nothing on faith.

Much the same can be said for technology. Where scientists are interested in understanding the nature of the world and how it and its parts work, technologists are interested in using that information. Where the scientist is interested in whether something is true, the technologist wants to know whether it works. For the purposes of this book, science can be taken to include technology, for the two are closely linked. To see how, consider the field of science known as optics, which involves passing light through lenses. Optical physicists approach it as science; opticians approach it as technology.

The word *science* itself comes from a Latin root that means simply "to know." We use it to describe knowledge that is collected and interpreted in a certain systematic way. We also use it for the process of collection and interpretation; that is, a "scientist" is one who "does science." We do not use the word *science* the same way we use the term *biology* or *physics*, to delimit a certain, restricted portion of the study of the world. Absolutely everything can (and does!) fall into the realm of science. (Even the study of illusory flying saucers, angels, "psychic" spoon benders, and ghosts—all said to be "beyond science"—belongs to the science of psychology.)

The key to science—skepticism—is what the scientific method is designed to support (see Figure 1.2). The point of the scientific method is to make it possible for each scientist's work to be checked by others. Work that can withstand such scrutiny is accepted as true and becomes part of the body of scientific knowledge.

The scientific method begins with the observation of unexplained facts. As the observer studies the observations, he or she sees interrelationships and patterns. The observer generalizes a pattern to cover unobserved facts and devises a tentative explanation of the pattern, a *hypothesis*. The observer then tests this hypothesis on new observations with a planned experiment. If the experiment fails to confirm the hypothesis, the observer must formulate a new hypothesis and conduct another experiment. If, however, the experiment confirms the hypothesis, then the hypothesis becomes part of the observer's stock of knowledge. Thorough, repeated confirmation, along with success in helping to explain new observations, promotes a hypothesis to the status of *theory*, principle, or law.

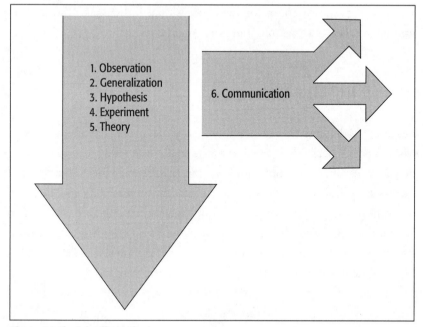

1. Observation
2. Generalization
3. Hypothesis
4. Experiment
5. Theory

6. Communication

Figure 1.2 The Scientific Method

One essential part of the scientific method is caution. Researchers go to great lengths to avoid the many kinds of error and bias that can contaminate experiments. They conduct controlled experiments to be sure that the results they see are real and not unforeseen effects of their experimental setups, and they analyze their results with statistics.

Another crucial part of the scientific method is communication. Observation, generalization, hypothesis, experiment, and theory are all useless if they are kept private. Even technicians, spending day after day on standardized tests of water quality or blood sugar levels, must record what they do and what they observe. A result is not a result—it has no validity, no credibility—if others cannot also obtain it; and others cannot seek it unless they know where and how to look. Thus, the scientific worker must publish scientific reports that explain observations, generalizations, hypotheses, and experiments in enough detail for others to repeat the work. Most of this communication still occurs in the traditional format of paper scientific journals, but scientists in many fields are now publishing in online electronic journals.

Science is thus firmly based on the notion of repeatability. It has little room for the unique or for those who keep their methods or findings secret, and even less room for those occasional individuals who invent fraudulent, false observations and experimental results.

SCIENCE AND ETHICS

Because this demand for repeatability means that every step of a scientist's work must be checkable, science possesses an accountability that other areas may lack. Anyone who contemplates a career in science must therefore be extremely ethical. Scientists must have a sense of responsibility and duty—a dedication to truth, accuracy, and completeness that supersedes all other loyalties. People with scientific training should find it difficult to conceal facts to protect their employer's financial or political interests. (They should find it difficult to protect their own interests in this way, too.)

A recent *New York Times* job market survey reported that students with both undergraduate and graduate technical degrees get the highest salary offers, especially, say hiring managers, if they show evidence that they can work well in teams, have strong ethics, do multiple tasks, and think strategically. The stress here on ethics is a good sign, but some employers seem to have other ideas, and too many scientists have lost their jobs because of their respect for truth. According to the Code of Ethics of the Association for Computing Machinery, ACM members should be prepared to put their jobs on the line in the service of ethics (see acm.org/constitution/code .html). For a helpful guide to the ethics of many fields, see http://onlineethics.org.

Most universities have ethics policies governing scientific research and carry out their own investigations of potential problems. In the U.S. Department of Health and Human Services, the Office of Research Integrity (http:// ori.dhhs.gov) "promotes integrity in biomedical and behavioral research supported by the Public Health Service (PHS) at about 4,000 institutions worldwide. ORI monitors institutional investigations of research misconduct." Scientists disciplined for unethical conduct may lose their jobs or be barred from receiving federal funding for their work.

Why would any scientist act unethically if the penalties can be so severe? Scientists are people, and they can have conflicting loyalties to employers, politics, religion, and even their own personal interests (fame and money). The demand for ethical behavior in science can thus present the scientist with a painful dilemma. So, too, can other high ideals. If it comforts you, take the pain as a measure of the ideal's worth. And remember that the world is far from perfect, that no ideal is shared by everyone, and that we must each live up to our own standards as best we can. Many of us manage to find relatively comfortable levels of compromise with our ideals.

SCIENCE AND SURVIVAL

Science is not dedicated to truth alone. The knowledge obtained by the scientific method has many valuable uses. It eases labor with new machines, processes, and materials. It aids health with medications and treatments. It improves the food supply. It finds new sources of energy and raw materials. It discovers that an asteroid struck Earth some 65 million years ago and destroyed the dinosaurs (among other species), and then it extends that insight to the realization that a nuclear war could have a very similar impact on us (a notion that has been credited with helping to end the Cold War). It identifies ecological crises, such as acid rain, carbon dioxide–induced climate change (global warming), and chlorofluorocarbon-caused damage to the ozone layer—crises that result in dying forests, rising sea levels, and increasing risk of skin cancer; and it tells us what to do to solve or adapt to these problems. It contributes to our understanding of how people act in groups and hence to our knowledge of how best to lead and govern.

A job serves the jobholder's individual survival. A career in science does that as well, but it also serves the survival of the human species. Success in such a career can provide immense personal satisfaction. No scientist has ever truly saved the world or the human species from destruction, but many who pursue careers in science have, as a result of their labors, saved or improved lives, fed the hungry, or warmed the cold. They have identified hazards, and they have found answers. They have made discoveries that spawned industries and employed thousands or even millions. They defend us all against the forces of extinction, and their dedication is that of the soldier in love with the battle. Scientists often say that they are the most blessed of human beings, because they are paid for doing what they would do as a hobby if they had to.

WHO ARE THE SCIENTISTS?

The people who follow careers in science are dedicated to truth and human survival. They are also dedicated to the search for knowledge. They live to wrest new facts from nature's grasp and to find new ways to use previously known facts. They seek the new in basic research; they use the old in applied research and in the myriad nonresearch jobs of technicians and engineers. Many also spread the word to students and the lay public by teaching and writing. Very few seek wealth, although applied researchers may come up with new products, drugs, devices, or production methods that pay off handsomely indeed. Occasionally, even basic researchers can find wealth, as did the pioneers of recombinant DNA. Here, the discovery of restriction enzymes that can cut and splice DNA strands at specific points made it immediately possible, for instance, to transplant genes from one organism to another and to grow human proteins in bacteria. Many of the basic researchers who first discovered how to do this are now associated with successful genetic engineering firms. Indeed, this basic knowledge has lead to a wealth of genetically modified organisms that resist herbicides, make their own insecticides, or have enhanced nutritional value.

THE SCIENTIST'S CHARACTER

Scientists seek knowledge, truth, and human survival using the scientific method. Potential scientists need the ability to work and think methodically. They must exhibit a number of other traits as well, for scientists in general are persistent, curious, creative, precise, intelligent, objective, honest, and enthusiastic. Very similar traits are prized in any workplace.

Persistence

Persistence means never giving up. Scientists seek answers to novel questions, and they try again and again and again when their attempts don't work out.

A classic example of persistence is the German scientist Paul Ehrlich, who tried 605 different drugs as cures for syphilis before he found the famed 606 in 1909. Better drugs now exist, but Ehrlich began the use of chemotherapy for disease. Today the development of a new drug may require the screening of thousands of candidates.

Curiosity

Curiosity is a very basic characteristic of the scientific personality. It is essential not only to basic and applied researchers, but also to the teachers who must encourage it in students; they teach best when they are models of the trait.

What is curiosity? It is the ability to be forever asking questions and seeking answers. The process of asking and answering need not be complicated, as one graduate student's experience shows. He was studying motor reflexes. One of these reflexes appears when cats mate, for the male always (or nearly always) bites the female in the back of the neck. In response, the female assumes an appropriate posture that facilitates mating. The graduate student asked: Is this reflex necessary to the act? Would blocking it prevent mating and perhaps offer a method of contraception for house cats? His answer: A cardboard shield constructed to cover the back of the female's neck did in fact prevent mating.

The willingness to try out new ideas is the aspect of curiosity that is essential to science. It is the essence of experiment.

Creativity

Many people believe that creativity is just for poets, novelists, sculptors, and other artists. But it is also essential for research scientists and teachers. Researchers need it to devise new hypotheses and the experiments with which to test them. Both researchers and teachers must be creative in how they express their results and knowledge if they are to communicate effectively with their peers, their students, and the general public.

Precision

Many scientists require a steady, precise hand for manipulating tiny objects, as in dissecting fruit flies or single cells or in repairing electronic equipment. All scientists need a precise mind for noting fine distinctions and avoiding subtle errors. Both mind and hand can be trained, and that is one aim of every college science lab.

Intelligence

Any scientist will find mental alertness, quickness, and agility useful in reaching the top, but genius is not absolutely necessary. Few people can or should set their sights on the Nobel Prize for their career objective. However, all should be able to reason abstractly and concretely, solve problems and comprehend new facts, and trade old notions for new. Intelligence is essential, but mental flexibility may be more important than high IQ.

Objectivity and Honesty

We have already noted that scientists must have a high regard for truth. That is, they must be honest. In addition, and in the service of honesty, they must be objective. They cannot let laziness, haste, or enchantment with their ideas keep them from testing their hypotheses with experiments. They cannot hide from critics by draping themselves in the holy cloak of science, believing that because they are scientists, they have a monopoly on truth—or that because they are scientists, whatever they say is the truth.

Objectivity requires the strength not to deceive the self. Konrad Lorenz once said it meant discarding a pet hypothesis every day before breakfast. Louis Flexner said, "Although I have great confidence in the observations, . . . the interpretations . . . badly need further work to test them."

The truly objective scientist rarely comes out decisively on one side of an issue. Quizzed before Congress, the scientist states an opinion, but then adds, "On the other hand . . . " For this reason, our representatives in Washington have more than once wished for a one-armed scientist.

Absolute objectivity is rare, and many nonscientists find it disturbing and even threatening. So do some scientists who fall short of their own ideals. It is often said, with some justice, that a truly new idea gains acceptance only with the death of the older members of the field who refuse to accept it.

Other Traits

Honesty, persistence, objectivity, curiosity, precision, creativity, and intelligence are all necessary traits for the scientist. Particular fields require other traits. Any scientist must have an enthusiasm for his or her own field. More today than ever before, scientists must be able to manage people (in research teams and in entrepreneurial start-up companies) and communicate well. A biologist must care about the animals, plants, and people on which he or she experiments and treat them humanely (only in studies of stress do distressed organisms yield trustworthy data). Outdoor specialists such as wildlife biologists, archaeologists, and geologists need stamina, strength, and outdoor experience. Others may require physical courage, tolerance for heat or cold, or the ability to fly a spacecraft or work in isolation or in crowds. Most specialties call for the ability to work well as part of a team, for modern science is very much a team effort. In physics and astronomy, research papers may have hundreds of names attached, to reflect the number of people involved in the research.

EMPLOYMENT IN SCIENCE AND ENGINEERING

According to the National Science Foundation's *Science and Engineering Indicators—2002,* in 1999 almost 11 million people had degrees related to science and engineering, but only about a third actually worked at jobs in science and engineering. Many worked in such fields as sales, management, administration, writing, and editing. At the same time, some people without science and engineering degrees do work in science and engineering. Altogether, the 1999 National Science Foundation (NSF) data show some 3.5 million people earning their living in science and engineering occupations.

The U.S. Department of Labor's Bureau of Labor Statistics looks more at actual occupations than degrees. Table 1.1 shows the numbers of people working as scientists and engineers in the year 2000. In 2000, there were 1,903,100 people employed as engineers, 2,253,000 employed as computer and information scientists, and 787,500 employed as physical, mathematical, life, and social scientists. These figures do not include university and college faculty (1.3 million people in both science and nonscience fields). Nor do these figures include those employed in nonscientific fields, which, according to the NSF, amount to over two-thirds of all those with science and engineering degrees.

Table 1.1 does not include many people who might quite reasonably be said to have science and engineering careers. Besides the medical scientists cited in Table 1.1, there were over 9 million additional people working in the medical field, including 3,337,300 technicians and technologists of various sorts, 2,200,000 registered nurses, 598,000 physicians and surgeons, and 59,000 veterinarians (see Table 1.2). In addition, there were 887,000 engineering, natural science, computer information system, and health services managers, and 1,247,000 nonmedical scientific technicians. It certainly seems reasonable to say that all these people enjoy careers in science, and their total number is well worth stressing. The numbers in Tables 1.1 and 1.2 add up to a total of 16,511,600 people (not counting college and university faculty) earning their living from science and engineering. This amounts to almost 12 percent of the 141 million people in the labor force in the United States in the year 2000.

The demand for scientists, engineers, and related personnel has increased steadily and dramatically for the last half century, despite the end

Table 1.1 Employment of Scientists and Engineers, 2000

SCIENTISTS AND ENGINEERS	TOTAL	4,943,600
Engineers	**Total**	**1,903,100**
Aerospace engineers		50,000
Agricultural engineers		2,400
Biomedical engineers		7,200
Chemical engineers		33,000
Civil engineers		232,000
Computer hardware engineers		60,000
Computer software engineers		697,000
Electrical and electronics (except computer) engineers		288,000
Environmental engineers		52,000
Industrial (including health and safety) engineers		198,000
Materials engineers		33,000
Mechanical engineers		221,000
Mining and geological (including mining safety) engineers		6,500
Nuclear engineers		14,000
Petroleum engineers		9,000
Scientists	**Total**	**3,040,500**
Physical scientists		**205,900**
Atmospheric scientists		6,900
Chemists and materials scientists		92,000
Environmental scientists and geoscientists		97,000
Physicists and astronomers		10,000
Mathematical scientists		**36,600**
Actuaries		14,000
Mathematicians		3,600
Statisticians		19,000
Computer and information scientists		**2,253,000**
Computer programmers		585,000
Computer support specialists and system administrators		734,000
Operations research analysts		47,000
Computer systems analysts		431,000
Network systems and data communications analysts		119,000
Database administrators		106,000
Computer and information scientists, research		28,000
Other computer specialists		203,000
Life scientists		**184,000**
Agricultural and food scientists		17,000
Biological and medical scientists		138,000
Conservation scientists and foresters		29,000
Social scientists		**361,000**
Economists and market and survey researchers		134,000
Psychologists		182,000
Anthropologists, archeologists, geographers, historians, political scientists, and sociologists		15,000
Urban and regional planners		30,000

Source: U. S. Department of Labor, Bureau of Labor Statistics, *Occupational Outlook Handbook*, 2002–2003 (Washington, DC: U. S. Department of Labor, Bureau of Labor Statistics, 2002).

Table 1.2 Nonscientists in the Sciences, 2000

NONSCIENTISTS IN THE SCIENCES	TOTAL 11,568,000
Health treatment and assessment	**4,347,000**
Chiropractors	50,000
Counselors	465,000
Dentists	152,000
Dietitians and nutritionists	49,000
Occupational therapists	78,000
Optometrists	31,000
Pharmacists	217,000
Physical therapists	132,000
Physician assistants	58,000
Physicians and surgeons	598,000
Podiatrists	18,000
Recreational therapists	29,000
Registered nurses	2,200,000
Respiratory therapists	110,000
Speech-language pathologists and audiologists	101,000
Veterinarians	59,000
Medical technicians	**5,087,000**
Cardiovascular technologists and technicians	39,000
Clinical laboratory technologists and technicians	295,000
Dental assistants	247,000
Dental hygienists	147,000
Dental laboratory technicians	43,000
Diagnostic medical sonographers	33,000
Dietetic technicians	26,000
Dispensing opticians	68,000
Emergency medical technicians	172,000
Licensed practical nurses	700,000
Medical record and health information technicians	136,000
Medical assistants	329,000
Nuclear medicine technologists	18,000
Nursing, psychiatric, and home health aides	2,100,000
Occupational safety and health specialists and technicians	35,000
Occupational therapy assistants and aides	25,000
Pharmacy aides	57,000
Pharmacy technicians	190,000
Physical therapy assistants and aides	86,000
Psychiatric technicians	54,000
Radiological technologists	167,000
Surgical technologists	71,000
Veterinary technicians	49,000

Table 1.2 Nonscientists in the Sciences, 2000, *continued*

Other technicians	**1,247,000**
Archivists, curators, and museum technicians	21,000
Drafters	213,000
Engineering technicians	519,000
Inspectors and compliance officers	175,000
Scientific technicians	198,000
Surveyors, cartographers, photogrammetrists, and surveying technicians	121,000
Managers	**887,000**
Computer and information systems managers	313,000
Engineering and natural sciences managers	324,000
Health services managers	250,000

Source: U. S. Department of Labor, Bureau of Labor Statistics, *Occupational Outlook Handbook*, 2002–2003 (Washington, DC: U. S. Department of Labor, Bureau of Labor Statistics, 2002).

of the Cold War, the downsizing in the 1990s of many firms that once employed large numbers of technical personnel, and the more recent failures of the so-called dot-coms (computer, Internet, and E-commerce businesses). According to the NSF's *Science and Engineering Indicators—2002*, science and engineering employment increased by 159 percent between 1980 and 2000, and "the most explosive growth was in mathematics and computer sciences, which experienced a 623 percent increase." The unemployment rate for science and engineering workers is typically low—only 1.6 percent in 1999, when the general unemployment rate was 4.4 percent.

The pattern is nicely reflected in U.S. federal research and development (R&D) expenditures, which were less than $10 billion in 1960 and are now over $100 billion. In the last few years, U.S. federal R&D spending has increased especially rapidly, with some year-to-year increases exceeding the 1960 total; see Table 1.3. The 2002 R&D budget was the first to exceed $100 billion. The Department of Defense's R&D budget topped $50 billion; the National Institutes of Health (NIH) got almost $23 billion; and terrorism-related R&D rose sharply to $1.5 billion. The 2003 R&D budget provided additional large increases for both health and defense-related R&D, with defense-related R&D taking the lead, largely as a result of post–September 11 (2001) concerns about national security, and surpassing the 1987 Cold War peak. In 2003, the new Department of Homeland Security was budgeted to spend about $800 million on science and technology in fiscal year 2004.

In Canada, research funding is more modest, and a larger share is left to the private sector, but the federal role has recently been increasing. As in the

Table 1.3 Federal R&D Funding, in Millions of Dollars (Current)

	2000	2001	2002	APPROVED 2003	PROPOSED 2004
TOTAL	**83,347**	**90,891**	**103,100**	**117,297**	**122,485**
Defense	**42,497**	**45,543**	**53,731**	**62,986**	**67,515**
Nondefense	**40,850**	**45,348**	**49,368**	**54,311**	**54,970**
Space	8,606	9,324	9,227	10,145	10,032
Health	18,689	21,422	24,748	28,315	28,971
Energy	1,282	1,381	1,332	1,366	1,374
General science	5,498	6,241	6,605	7,025	7,375
Natural resources and environment	2,070	2,199	2,175	2,249	2,210
Agriculture	1,479	1,716	1,909	1,924	1,693
Transportation	1,815	1,675	1,889	1,689	1,881
Commerce	479	471	549	563	424
International	172	140	279	301	306
All other	760	779	656	734	704

Source: American Association for the Advancement of Science, Budget and Policy Program (www.aaas.org/spp/rd).

United States, policy makers see R&D funds as an investment in creating new industries (such as information technology and biotechnology), creating related jobs, and motivating people interested in science and technology careers to remain in Canada instead of going abroad (especially to the United States). In 2000–2001, a third of the Canadian government's expenditures on science activities went to Environment Canada, the National Research Council, the Natural Sciences and Engineering Research Council, and Statistics Canada. The Medical Research Council, the Natural Sciences and Engineering Research Council, the Social Sciences and Humanities Research Council, and the Canada Foundation for Innovation dispensed 88 percent of federal funding for the university sector. In 2002, Health Minister Anne McClellan said that she expected to increase the Canadian Institutes of Health's research funding from $560 million to $1 billion by 2005. The Canada Foundation for Innovation also announced increased funding for science and engineering research.

Changes in technology have always meant some loss of jobs. For instance, the rise of information technology—especially personal computers and office networks—has meant less need for word processors, typists, computer operators, and telephone operators, among other occupations expected to decline significantly by 2010.

However, many scientific and technical occupations do appear on the Bureau of Labor Statistics' list of fastest-growing occupations, which is dominated by computer specialists and health-care workers. Many more science and technology occupations appear on the Department of Labor's breakdown of fastest-growing occupations according to the amount of education they require (see Table 1.4). Some jobs (for example, in health care) reflect an aging population. Others reflect changes in technology (information technology and biotechnology). Many jobs are expected to become available as present employees retire. The job prospects for those with a scientific-technical education—especially in computer and health-related areas—look excellent.

Most scientists and engineers are employed by business and industry in research and development, production, environmental monitoring, mineral exploration, and other activities. This will undoubtedly continue to be the case. The areas of greatest growth will be determined by the ongoing development (and penetration into government, industry, and the home) of information and communications technologies and by the development of new technologies, such as biological engineering (including genetic engineering and cloning) and nanotechnology. Other areas will be spurred by the efforts to cope with problems such as global climate change, an ever-growing population, new diseases, and the aging of the American population. You will note that several of the items listed here are "environmental." According to one count, by 1997, environmental concerns and regulations were responsible for more than 11 million jobs worldwide.

Educational institutions and the federal government employ fewer scientists and engineers, but as noted earlier, federal R&D funding is increasing. This should lead to increased employment opportunities, as should the large number of retirements expected over the coming decade or two.

In 1999, about 12 percent of the science and engineering workforce was foreign-born. At the doctoral level, the percentage was 27 percent. In the interests of homeland security, the federal government in 2002 began restricting visas for foreign students and even for visiting scientists. If this continues, demand for American science and engineering workers will rise sharply.

It is worth noting that the doctorate is by no means essential for a career in science. Overall, most working scientists and engineers have only a bachelor's

Table 1.4 Education Needed for the Fastest Growing Occupations, 2000–2010

EDUCATION REQUIRED	FASTEST GROWING OCCUPATIONS (in Percent)	FASTEST GROWING OCCUPATIONS (in Numbers)
First professional degree	Veterinarians Pharmacists Chiropractors Optometrists	Physicians and surgeons Pharmacists Veterinarians
Doctoral degree	Computer & information scientists, research Medical scientists Postsecondary teachers Biological scientists Astronomers & physicists	Postsecondary teachers Biological scientists Computer & information scientists, research Medical scientists Astronomers & physicists
Master's degree	Audiologists Speech-language pathologists Mental health & substance-abuse social workers Substance abuse & behavioral disorder counselors Physical therapists	Educational, vocational, & school counselors Physical therapists Speech-language pathologists Psychologists Mental health & substance-abuse social workers
Bachelor's degree or higher, plus work experience	Computer & information systems managers Medical & health services managers	Computer & information systems managers
Bachelor's degree	Computer software engineers, applications Computer software engineers, systems software Network & computer systems administrators Network systems & data communications analysts Database administrators	Computer software engineers, applications Computer software engineers, systems software Computer systems analysts Network & computer systems administrators
Associate degree	Computer support specialists Medical records & health information technicians Physical therapist assistants Occupational therapist assistants Veterinary technologists & technicians	Registered nurses Computer support specialists Medical records & health information technicians Dental hygienists
On-the-job training (1–12 months)	Medical assistants Dental assistants Pharmacy technicians	Medical assistants

Source: U. S. Department of Labor, Bureau of Labor Statistics, *Occupational Outlook Handbook*, 2002–2003 (Washington, DC, U. S. Department of Labor, Bureau of Labor Statistics, 2002).

degree; this is certainly the case for computer scientists and mathematicians. Life and medical scientists tend to have doctorates or professional (for example, M.D.) degrees, as do social scientists. Physical scientists tend to have doctorates.

We will look at pay scales later in this book, but we should note here that pay varies by field as well as by academic degree. Table 1.5 gives the median salaries for several occupations. Of course, starting pay is less than the median, which covers both novice and experienced workers, but it varies in much the same way. You might note that engineering and computer sciences offer the best pay for those with no more than a bachelor's degree; these fields also have a high demand for new graduates.

We will look at projections for job openings later in this book, when we consider specific careers in the various fields. For now it will suffice to observe that overall demand for science and engineering personnel is expected to rise by 47 percent, or 2.2 million jobs, about three times as rapidly as for all occupations through 2010. A career in science and engineering is therefore a fairly reliable route to job and economic security and hence personal and family survival. Because these careers also serve the cause of human survival on—and perhaps eventually off—this planet, they also offer a sense of mission, a dedication that makes life worth living. And, of course, science encompasses the most fascinating, absorbing, and challenging of topics. It is not for everyone, but for those who embrace it, science holds immense personal—and often financial—satisfaction.

Table 1.5 Median Annual Salaries of U.S. Individuals in Science & Engineering Occupations, 1999

	AVERAGE SALARY
All S&E employees	$60,000
Computer/math scientists	64,000
Life and related scientists	47,700
Physical and related scientists	52,000
Social and related scientists	47,000
Engineers	65,000

Source: National Science Board, *Science and Engineering Indicators, 2002* (Arlington, VA: National Science Foundation, 2002) NSB-02-1.

WOMEN AND MINORITIES

What's the story for women and minorities? Despite years of effort, there remains a problem. The percentages of men and women who have at least a high school education are nearly equal today, and the proportion of women with college degrees is rapidly approaching that for men (see Table 1.6). Racial disparities are greater than gender disparities, for fewer blacks—and still fewer Hispanics—complete high school and go on to obtain college and graduate degrees.

According to the National Science Foundation, even though women make up almost half the U.S. workforce (46.5 percent) and a slightly greater proportion of the college-degreed workforce (48.6 percent in 2000), they make up no more than a quarter of those employed in science and engineering (24.7 percent in 2000). The disparity is marked, but we must recognize that 24.7 percent is half again the comparable 1993 figure and more than double the 1980 figure (11.6 percent).

Asians make up 11 percent of the science and engineering workforce even though they are only 4 percent of the overall population. Blacks, Hispanics, and Native Americans together make up 24 percent of the population but only 7 percent of the science and engineering workforce. Blacks and Hispanics have also more than doubled their participation in the science and engineering workforce since 1980. Blacks make up 7.4 percent of the college-degreed workforce and 3 percent of the science and engineering workforce (up from 2.6 percent in 1980). Hispanics make up 4.3 percent of the college-degreed workforce and 3.2 percent of the science and engineering workforce (up from 2.0 percent in 1980).

Clearly, there has been improvement, but whites and males still dominate science and engineering. In addition, whites and males enjoy lower unemployment rates in science and engineering and are more likely to be employed full-time and in the fields of their degrees. They also earn more (see Table 1.7). The greatest disparities are between male and female and between white and black. According to a 2002 salary survey conducted by Abbott, Langer & Associates (paysurvey.com/alasci.html; reported in *The Scientist*, September 16, 2002), in the life sciences, for instance, women earn 6 to 24 percent less than men, and blacks earn 16 to 24 percent less than whites.

Table 1.6 Educational Attainment by Race and Gender (in Percent)

YEAR	ALL RACES		WHITE		BLACK		ASIAN AND PACIFIC ISLANDER		HISPANIC	
	Male	Female	Male	Female	Male	Female	Male	Female	Male	Female
High School Graduate or More										
1960	39.5	42.5	41.6	44.7	18.2	21.8	(NA)	(NA)	(NA)	(NA)
1970	51.9	52.8	54.0	55.0	30.1	32.5	(NA)	(NA)	37.9	34.2
1980	67.3	65.8	69.6	68.1	50.8	51.5	(NA)	(NA)	67.3	65.8
1990	77.7	77.5	79.1	79.0	65.8	66.5	84.0	77.2	50.3	51.3
2000	84.2	84.0	84.8	85.0	78.7	78.3	88.2	83.4	56.6	57.5
College Graduate or More										
1960	9.7	5.8	10.3	6.0	2.8	3.3	(NA)	(NA)	(NA)	(NA)
1965	12.0	7.1	12.7	7.3	4.9	4.5	(NA)	(NA)	(NA)	(NA)
1970	13.5	8.1	14.4	8.4	4.2	4.6	(NA)	(NA)	7.8	4.3
1975	17.6	10.6	18.4	11.0	6.7	6.2	(NA)	(NA)	8.3	4.6
1980	20.1	12.8	21.3	13.3	8.4	8.3	(NA)	(NA)	9.4	6.0
1985	23.1	16.0	24.0	16.3	11.2	11.0	(NA)	(NA)	9.7	7.3
1990	24.4	18.4	25.3	19.0	11.9	10.8	44.9	35.4	9.8	8.7
2000	27.8	23.6	28.5	23.9	16.3	16.7	47.6	40.7	10.7	10.6

NA: not available

Source: U.S. Department of Commerce, U. S. Census Bureau, *Statistical Abstract of the United States: 2001* (Washington, DC: U. S. Census Bureau, 2002).

Table 1.7 Median Annual Salaries of U.S. Individuals in Science and Engineering Occupations by Gender and Race, 1999

	AVERAGE SALARY
All S&E employees	$60,000
Male	64,000
Female	50,000
White	61,000
Black	53,000
Hispanic	55,000
Asian/Pacific Islander	62,000
Other	52,000

Source: U. S. Department of Labor, Bureau of Labor Statistics, *Occupational Outlook Handbook, 2002–2003* (Washington, DC: U. S. Department of Labor, Bureau of Labor Statistics, 2002).

Women have long been most heavily represented in the social and life sciences and least represented in engineering. This has not changed, though in the last decade women have increased their proportion of engineers to 10 percent. However, the proportion of women in the computer sciences has actually declined. Asians are heavily represented in the physical and computer sciences, blacks in the social and computer sciences and mathematics, and Native Americans in the social and life sciences. Hispanics are more evenly distributed across disciplines.

Overall, the figures for women and minorities indicate considerable improvement in employment patterns over the last few decades, thanks to a concerted effort to bring a more diverse group onto educational tracks leading to scientific careers and also because of the effort to overcome the institutional and social barriers that have long restricted women and minorities to service and low-level jobs. Unfortunately, equal opportunity still has a long way to go, and the problem is in large part self-perpetuating, for there are few women and minority role models to convince young people that they, too, can attain positions in science and engineering. Moreover, the lack of women and minorities in most scientific and technical fields makes it very easy for guidance counselors, parents, and young people to think that those fields are inappropriate or unwelcoming for women, blacks, Hispanics, and others. The truth, of course, is quite the opposite.

Women and minorities have just as much potential as white males to be physicists, physicians, computer scientists, astronomers, engineers—in short, whatever kind of scientist they want to be.

Information Sources and Assistance for Women and Minorities Interested in Science Careers

The American Indian Science and Engineering Society (AISES)
P.O. Box 9828
Albuquerque, NM 87119-9828
www.aises.org

Math, Engineering, Science Achievement (MESA)
Chancellor's Office
California Community Colleges
1102 Q Street
Sacramento, CA 95814-6511
www.cccco.edu/divisions/esed/irt/mesa.htm

National Action Council for Minorities in Engineering Inc. (NACME)
350 Fifth Avenue, Suite 2212
New York, NY 10118-2299
www.nacme.org

National Association for Equal Opportunity in Higher Education
8701 Georgia Avenue, Suite 200
Silver Spring, MD 20910
www.nafeo.org/index.html

National Institutes of Health
Black Scientists Association
P.O. Box 2262
Kensington, MD 20891-2262
www.bsa.od.nih.gov

National Organization for the Professional Advancement of Black
  Chemists and Chemical Engineers (NOBCChE)
P.O. Box 77040 Washington, DC 20013
www.nobcche.org

National Science Foundation
Division of Human Resource Development
4201 Wilson Boulevard, Suite 815
Arlington, VA 22230
www.ehr.nsf.gov/ehr/hrd

Quality Education for Minorities Network
1818 N Street, NW, Suite 350
Washington, DC 20036
www.qemnetwork.qem.org

Society for the Advancement of Chicanos and
Native Americans in Science (SACNAS)
P.O. Box 8526
Santa Cruz, CA 95061
www.sacnas.org

Society of Women Engineers
230 E. Ohio Street, Suite 400
Chicago, IL 60611-3265
www.swe.org

Women in Science and Engineering (WiSE)
102 Wilson Annex
University of Washington
P.O. Box 352135
Seattle, WA 98195-2135
www.engr.washington.edu/~uwwise

2

CHOOSING A FIELD OF SCIENCE

It seems reasonable to assume that anyone reading a book called *Careers in Science* must already have chosen a life in science. That is, you must already find fascinating the thought of probing the unknown faces of nature or using the results of such probing to aid human health, build new devices or structures, or contribute to the world in some other way. You must believe you have the intelligence, creativity, objectivity, curiosity, and persistence to be a scientist or scientific worker of some kind. Perhaps you want to contribute to the survival of humanity in what many think is the most valuable way, by anticipating and solving the problems that arise from life on a small planet.

Many people who choose science—or even one particular field of science—early in life pursue education to the limits of their ability, patience, and funds. Then they take whatever job they can find in the field they have studied most. That first job leads to others and becomes a career. Yet that career can be haphazard. It is far, far better to gather all available information at an early stage. Make an informed choice, and plan. Begin by learning what interests, abilities, and personalities match up with which fields of science. Learn what level of education is necessary for the career that seems to fit best. Learn where to go for that education and how to fund it.

That knowledge is the fruit you can expect to reap from this book. Let's begin by looking at a simple, easily accessible personality assessment test. We will then consider John Holland's classic work on personality types and their relevance to career selection.

PERSONALITY AND CAREER CHOICE

The Myers-Briggs personality assessment uses an individual's responses to a series of questions to measure where he or she falls on four ranges, or scales. These scales are extroversion–introversion; sensing–intuitive; thinking–feeling; and judging–perceptive. One's score is expressed as a four-letter sequence, such as INTJ (introverted, intuitive, thinking, judging). Each possible score is accompanied by an interpretative paragraph. For instance, a young woman with an INTJ score supposedly has an original mind and a great drive for her own ideas and purposes and is skeptical, critical, independent, determined, and often stubborn; in a field that appeals to her, she can organize a job and carry it through with or without help.

The Myers-Briggs test is designed to be administered by trained professionals. A rough do-it-yourself approximation is available at teamtechnology .co.uk/tt/h-articl/mb-simpl.htm. A related test is the Keirsey Temperament Sorter, available online at http://keirsey.com.

The Myers-Briggs and Keirsey scores have a certain obvious, though vague, relevance to career choices. However, in their reliance on only four scales, the tests underrate the true complexity of personality so severely that they are far too oversimplified to be very useful. Their one advantage is that versions of the tests are readily available on the Internet.

John Holland's approach allows a much more complex analysis of personality. According to Holland, people can be characterized in terms of six different personality types:

1. Realistic (R)—interested in mechanical and physical activities; a tool user; "strong" and "masculine," not socially skilled or sensitive
2. Investigative (I)—interested in thinking, organizing, and understanding; analytical, intellectual, curious, reserved, and scientific, not persuasive or social
3. Social (S)—interested in helping, teaching, and serving others; gregarious, friendly, cooperative, and tactful, not mechanical or technical
4. Conventional (C)—interested in orderly, structured situations with clear guidelines; precise, accurate, clerical, and conforming

5. Enterprising (E)—interested in organizing, directing, persuading, and exercising authority; persuasive, ambitious, and optimistic; a leader

6. Artistic (A)—interested in performing in sports or arts; emotional, aesthetic, autonomous, unconventional, impulsive, and imaginative

It is hard to think of any person whose personality does not fit this scheme, although almost no one is a pure realistic, investigative, social, conventional, enterprising, or artistic type. People's personalities tend to be predominantly of one type, with components of the others.

The same is true of jobs and careers. Scientists in general must be strongly investigative, but the best scientists are often artistic as well. Social scientists and teachers are also social. The heads of laboratories and academic departments and other managers are also enterprising. Engineers are investigative and realistic; mathematicians, investigative and conventional (and perhaps artistic); technicians, realistic and conventional.

Holland has devised a test, the Self-Directed Search (SDS), that anyone looking for a career can use (a version is available—but not free!—online at self-directed-search.com). The SDS permits the user to generate numerical measures of his or her personality in terms of Holland's six types. That is, a user of the SDS might find that the realistic component of his or her personality measures R = 40, while the other components come in at I = 32, S = 18, C = 30, E = 3, and A = 15. The top three measures then become a summary code, here RIC.

The SDS can be used with Holland's Occupations Finder, which lists over 1,300 occupations by three-letter codes, each code corresponding to a summary code. To use the Finder, one looks up the occupations listed under one's summary code (RIC in our example) and its permutations (RCI, IRC, ICR, CRI, and CIR). Holland then suggests that the user double-check his or her personality ratings by talking to others who know the user well and by making sure that potential occupations offer appealing lifestyles (do they involve travel? long hours? working with—or away from—other people?) and that he or she has the ability to undergo the necessary training. The user should also check out the occupations themselves by talking to people employed in these careers and reading career books such as the McGraw-Hill/Contemporary guides. College students may investigate a potential occupation by taking a part-time or summer job in it. A career counselor may also prove helpful.

OTHER FACTORS AFFECTING CAREER CHOICE

Personality type is only one of many factors that go into choosing a career. It is clearly important, though, for people tend to choose careers compatible with their personality. If they make a wrong choice, or if their personality changes to lessen compatibility, they may well change their career. It is no rarity for a businessperson to chuck it all in his or her forties, move to a rural area, and become an artist—or for an artist to go into business. Often, such changes come as a result of a "midlife crisis," when people realize they are not doing what truly fits them best.

Also important are interests, abilities, past exposures, models, and ambitions. All of these affect career choices, and all play a part when someone who has chosen the broad field of science narrows that choice down to mathematics, engineering, chemistry, biology, and so on. People choose a field of science in which to work after exposure, in high school or college courses or in part-time jobs, to several possibilities. One field proves most interesting, or it promises a more thorough use of one's talents, or it offers more (or less) exposure to people or machines or wildlife. It may be the field of a favorite teacher, relative, or family friend.

People choose their career within a field according to their ambitions, imagined roles, and capacities for responsibility and education. The career itself then develops with changing interests, further education and training, and promotions. Remember that a career is a sequence of positions.

THE FIELDS OF SCIENCE

It is possible to split up the broad area of science in several ways. The broadest split is that between *basic* (or "pure") and *applied* science. Basic science, or basic research, investigates the unknown, seeking new knowledge with little or no regard for its potential uses. Basic science is often justified with the argument that *all* knowledge, no matter how useless or irrelevant it may seem at first, eventually proves valuable. This argument has certainly proved right before. Work on large numbers has given rise to "unbreakable" codes. Studies of fungi and bacteria have resulted in the discovery of antibiotics. Research on insect communication by pheromones (odorous substances resembling hormones in function) has yielded new methods of pest control. Work on the behavior of electrons in semiconductors has given us the transistor and other electronic devices—and thus made possible the modern personal computer. The argument may well prove right again. The only real problem with it is that it requires the long view, and those to whom basic research must usually be justified are forced (by their need for profit or votes) to focus on the short term.

Applied research rarely needs justification. It focuses on ways to use the results of previous basic work, or it seeks answers to specific problems. For example, we see it in efforts to decrease the pollutant emissions of automobile engines, develop weapons from lasers, improve crop yields, tailor new crops, identify the causes of and solutions to global warming, and identify the causes and treatments of new diseases. In each case, there is a clear need and a direction in which to look for the answer to that need.

Applied scientists are not only researchers, however. Engineers follow principles of design to build safe structures. They may use new materials or construct devices never seen before, such as rocket engines and satellites, but they are also users of a body of established knowledge. So are the technicians who perform the numerous tests on which medicine, environmental monitoring, and industrial quality control depend. So are the mathematicians and statisticians who compute actuarial tables, analyze census figures, and make sense of the nation's economy. So, too, are computer programmers, mineral prospectors, and weather forecasters. Perhaps the main difference between these people and the applied researchers lies in the size of the problems they tackle and in the degree of uncertainty they face. Engineers, technicians, and the rest generally know just what methods to use (the methods may even be specified in a "cookbook," or handbook). Applied researchers must often develop the methods they need. They know only what they need the methods for, while basic researchers may not know even that.

The basic versus applied distinction can be quite helpful to people who are trying to decide on a career in science. How much direction do you need? How much uncertainty can you tolerate in your work? Choose accordingly, and then look at another way of splitting up science: according to topic areas, or the "fields of science." These are the specialties, and they distinguish scientists according to the aspects of nature that they focus on. By splitting science into specialties, we may fail to recognize the ways the fields overlap and build walls between specialties that require special effort to surmount. Still, this approach is useful both to the young person looking for a career and to the administrator trying to make a multifield institution, such as a university, function smoothly.

Helping Sciences

All sciences are "helping sciences," for all help our kind and others to survive. However, some are more particularly or more directly helpful than others; they help individuals, and they help very much in the short term— in minutes, hours, days, at most a lifetime. The helping sciences include human and veterinary medicine, the allied health professions, psychiatry, clinical psychology, and social work. They treat, ease, cure, and prevent physical and mental illness. They deal also with the poor, the retarded, the handicapped, and the elderly, who may not suffer from illness but do still need helping hands.

Social Sciences

Like the helping sciences, the social sciences deal mostly with people. They approach them in groups, though, and they take a larger, more long-term view. These sciences include sociology, cultural anthropology, political science, economics, and social psychology. Their aim is to explain how people behave en masse, in small groups and large, and to explicate culture and politics, war and peace, even crime and morality.

Life Sciences

The life sciences deal with the phenomena of life. They are the branches of biology—anatomy, botany, ethology, forestry, genetics, herpetology, immunology, physiology, toxicology, virology, zoology, and many, many more. Some touch on nonbiological fields, such as physics and chemistry, but only as these fields pertain to life. Others overlap with the helping and social sciences, as they pertain to animals, singly and in groups, as well as humans; their aim is to build overall schemes that put human behavior in an evolutionary, biological context. Still others, such as pharmacy, relate to medicine, but medicine is merely biology applied to questions of health. Controversy surrounds some areas, such as genetic engineering, which redesigns living things by putting in them genes from other species, as when crop plants are given genes that let them make their own insecticide or resist the effect of herbicides.

Does life fascinate you? Then perhaps you should become a biologist. What kind of biologist? Are you most interested in plants, animals, bacteria, or viruses? In reptiles, fish, birds, or mammals? In structure or function? In inheritance? In fossils or agriculture or behavior? Whatever your answer, biology has a branch for you. There are even two fields for the science fiction fan: space biology deals with the reactions of earthly organisms to the space environment; exobiology is the theory (no real data yet) of extraterrestrial life.

Earth Sciences

The earth sciences study the planet Earth. Geologists consider the planet's structure and history, as revealed in its rocks. Geochemists focus on the chemical processes responsible for rock and ore body formation. Geophysicists look at the larger processes that have folded rock layers and moved the plates of Earth's crust about. Their payoff is an understanding of the human species' only home, as well as better knowledge of how and where to find oil, gas, metal, and other raw materials essential to civilization.

The earth sciences also include oceanography, which focuses on the oceans, their bottoms and waters, their sediments and currents; and meteorology, which examines the atmosphere. Both fields strive to understand and predict winds and storms and rains and to forecast changes in heat and nutrient flow that affect fisheries. Both feed into the field of climatology (as do the space and other earth sciences), where fluctuations in ocean temperature, solar output, jet stream paths, volcanic dust clouds, and more are integrated to understand and predict the planet's climate.

Physical Sciences

The physical sciences deal with nonliving matter. Chemistry is one, with its chief branches of analytical, physical, organic, and inorganic chemistry and biochemistry. Speaking very broadly, chemistry studies the way atoms and molecules interact. Its discoveries yield fuels, fertilizers, plastics, pesticides, and adhesives. It warned us of the disastrous effects of carbon dioxide on world climate and of chlorofluorocarbons on the ozone layer. Traditionally dependent on the laboratory and the test tube, it now leans almost as heavily on computer simulation as we strive to understand how catalysts work and to design better catalysts, ionic traps, filters, and more.

Physics is another of the physical sciences, and it includes chemistry in its purview. At one extreme, physics studies the behavior of matter in bulk—the flow of fluids and the movement of objects affected by changing forces, such as friction and inertia. At the other extreme, it studies atoms and their constituent parts. Its results yield nuclear reactors and bombs, novel electronic devices, high-temperature superconductors, photovoltaic devices for solar power, and turbines that withstand the strains of high winds, strong water currents, and flight. Researchers in physics also contribute on a very fundamental level to chemistry, biology, astronomy, and geology.

Caught between chemistry and physics is materials science. Within its purview are the substances we use to make things. It pays great attention to surfaces, strengths, and durabilities, and it contributes to engineering.

Space Sciences

Astronomy is the first space science that comes to mind. Its subject is the classification, movement, and nature of the stars and planets. It is the science of telescopes, optical and radio, visual and—these days—electronic, on the ground and in orbit. Other fields include astrophysics, which strives at great distances to grasp the processes that generate and operate dust clouds, stars, and planets, and cosmology, whose aim is to know how all things began.

There's more. With the excursions of the Viking and Mariner and Pioneer probes was born the field of planetology, in essence the "earth sciences" of alien worlds, based on photographs, radar, and limited samples. There is astronautics, the science and art of building and guiding spacecraft. There's also space biology, exobiology (the theory of extraterrestrial life), and space medicine.

At the moment, the space sciences do not employ a great many people, but our species stands poised on the verge of a great leap outward. We are now capable of moving into space, of building colonies in orbit and setting others on hostile, alien worlds. There are signs that we may do these things —or some of them—within our own lifetime. The future may well need a great many space scientists, especially in astronautics and space biology and medicine, in the still unformed fields of orbital engineering and low-gravity agriculture, and maybe even in exobiology and extraterrestrial anthropology, psychology, and sociology. Eventually, we may undertake to make Mars more like Earth; then we will need planetary engineers to "terraform" the planet into livability.

Engineering

Engineers are humanity's builders and makers. They design and oversee the construction of cars, trains, ships, aircraft, and spacecraft, of farm equipment, highways, buildings, factories, and mines. They develop artificial organs, ceramics, metal alloys, and mechanisms. They are in great demand, essential, and well paid.

Mathematics and Computer Science

Computer science blends mathematics and electronic engineering. It adds cognitive psychology to its studies of artificial intelligence, and it rests firmly on logic and philosophy in its programming aspect. Like engineering, it is highly applied, in great demand, and well paid. It is also essential, for computers are now omnipresent in businesses, homes, and schools, being used for writing, calculating, data processing, communicating (via e-mail and chat), learning, games, and shopping. The most popular uses involve the Internet; over half the U.S. population and over a tenth of the world population had Internet access in 2002.

Mathematics, either pure or applied, is the systematic manipulation of numbers, magnitudes, and symbols. It is arithmetic, algebra, geometry, and calculus, measurement and statistics, modeling and projection. Mathematics is necessary in every field of science and business, but it is far less glamorous than computer science. Pure mathematics is largely an academic pursuit—the study of number theory, abstract algebra, and the like. Applied mathematics is very practical, finding niches in the insurance industry (actuaries), government (statisticians), and science and industry in general (measurers, calculators, modelers, and theoreticians). Its value to cryptography means that jobs exist in military, security, and intelligence agencies. Its value as a form of logic and its close relation to the computer sciences have led to the field of systems analysis, essential to modern decision making.

HAVE YOU CHOSEN?

Have you chosen your field of science yet? Basic or applied? The helping or social sciences? Biology or chemistry? Physics or the earth sciences? A future in space or engineering? Mathematics, perhaps? Or computers?

You may indeed already have a strong sense of where your future lies. However, do not make a final choice just yet. That must hinge on a deeper acquaintance with specific careers, which you will begin to gain later in this book. It may also depend on your capacity and inclination for education, for different careers call for different degrees, and the highest levels may require years of schooling and training.

Chapter 3 will outline the educational requirements and expenses of careers in science. It will not attempt to prescribe specific schools for specific fields, but it will point to some of the many available sources of financial aid.

THE RIGHT JOB

Many young people are interested in science, but they have little idea of just what they would like to spend their lives doing in science. One way to narrow down the options is to look at the job requirements (such as initiative, leadership, or stamina), the work environment (hazardous, outdoors, or confined), and the occupational characteristics (pay, entry requirements, and opportunities) of various scientific and technical jobs and consider how they match the budding scientist's, engineer's, or technician's personality, interests, and educational ambitions.

Table 2.1 on page 37 lists 78 jobs categorized by 17 job requirements, work environment features, and occupational characteristics.

Job Requirements

1. Leadership/persuasion—organizing others, supervising, directing
2. Helping/instructing others—treating, teaching, listening, counseling
3. Problem solving/creativity—designing, inventing, drawing, writing, and developing ideas or programs
4. Initiative—determining what needs to be done and completing jobs without close supervision
5. Working as part of a team—interacting cooperatively toward shared goals
6. Frequent public contact—dealing with the public on a regular basis
7. Manual dexterity—operating tools, testing, drafting, and so on
8. Physical stamina—enduring long-term stress and strain (for example, heavy lifting)

Work Environment

9. Hazardous—working with infectious materials or where accidents are common (such jobs require careful attention to safety precautions)
10. Outdoors—spending a major portion of the workday outdoors, usually without regard to weather
11. Confined—staying in a specific place for most of the workday

Occupational Characteristics

12. Geographically concentrated—50 percent or more of the jobs in five or fewer states
13. Part-time—often requiring less than thirty-five hours per week

14. Median annual earnings, 2000 (in thousands)

15. Employment growth—L = lowest; M = middle; H = highest; D = decline; based on projected growth to 2010)

16. Number of new jobs, 2000–2010 (in thousands)—usually much less than the number of job openings created by the need to replace workers who change occupations or leave the labor force

17. Entry requirements—L = a high school education or less, with basics often learned on the job; M = post–high school training, such as apprenticeship or junior college, or many months or years of experience; H = four or more years of college (usually)

A chemist needs more than a college education, must be able to solve problems and show initiative, and can expect moderate job prospects and high earnings. Engineers also need to be able to solve problems and show initiative, but they typically work in teams. In some specialties, the work is geographically concentrated. In most specialties, the job and earnings prospects are quite high. Table 2.1 provides an equivalent amount of information for many other jobs, and it makes abundantly clear that there is something in science for almost everyone who cares to look.

Table 2.1 Matching Yourself with the World of Work

OCCUPATION	JOB REQUIREMENTS								WORK ENVIRONMENT				OCCUPATIONAL CHARACTERISTICS				
	1*	2*	3*	4	5*	6*	7*	8*	9*	10*	11*	12*	13*	14*	15*	16*	17*
Engineers/Surveyors/Architects																	
Architects			•	•	•	•	•							52	M	19	H
Surveyors	•				•		•	•		•				37	M	20	M
Engineers																	
Aerospace engineers			•	•	•							•		68	M	7	H
Agricultural engineers			•	•	•									56	M	0.4	H
Biomedical engineers			•	•	•									57	H	2.3	H
Chemical engineers			•	•	•									66	L	1.4	H
Civil engineers			•	•	•									56	M	24	H
Computer hardware engineers			•	•	•									67	H	15	H
Computer software engineers			•	•	•									68	H	664	H
Electrical/electronics engineers			•	•	•									65	M	31	H
Environmental engineers			•	•	•									58	H	14	H
Industrial engineers			•	•	•									59	L	12	H
Materials engineers			•	•	•									59	L	1.8	H
Mechanical engineers			•	•	•									59	M	25	H
Mining/geological engineers			•	•	•									61	M	−0.1	H
Nuclear engineers			•	•	•									79	L	0.3	H
Petroleum engineers			•	•	•							•		79	D	−0.6	H

*1. Leadership/persuasion
*2. Helping/instructing others
*3. Problem solving/creativity
*4. Initiative
*5. Working as part of a team
*6. Frequent public contact
*7. Manual dexterity
*8. Physical stamina

*9. Hazardous
*10. Outdoors
*11. Confined
*12. Geographically concentrated
*13. Part-time
*14. Median annual earnings, 2000 (in thousands)
*15. Employment growth

*16. Number of new jobs, 2000–2010 (in thousands)
*17. Entry requirements (cols.15 & 17):
    H = hard
    M = medium
    L = low
    D = decline

Source: Adapted and updated from Melvin Fountain, "Matching Yourself with the World of Work," *Occupational Outlook Quarterly* (Fall 1986). Updated data from *Occupational Outlook Handbook, 2002–2003* (Washington, DC: U.S. Department of Labor, Bureau of Labor Statistics, 2002) and *Occupational Outlook Quarterly* (Spring 2002).

Table 2.1 *Continued*

OCCUPATION	JOB REQUIREMENTS								WORK ENVIRONMENT				OCCUPATIONAL CHARACTERISTICS				
	1*	2*	3*	4	5*	6*	7*	8*	9*	10*	11*	12*	13*	14*	15*	16*	17*
Scientists/Mathematicians																	
Computer/Mathematical Occupations																	
Accountants/auditors		•	•		•	•					•			44	M	181	H
Actuaries			•	•							•	•		67	L	0.8	H
Computer programmers			•		•						•			58	M	95	H
Computer scientists/ systems analysts database administrators	•	•	•	•	•						•			59	H	554	H
Computer support specialists/ system administrators	•	•	•	•	•						•			36	H	667	H
Mathematicians			•	•										69	D	−0.1	H
Operations research analysts	•	•	•	•	•						•			53	L	3.8	H
Statisticians			•	•										52	L	0.5	H
Physical Scientists																	
Atmospheric scientists			•	•	•									59	M	1.2	H
Chemists/materials scientists			•	•										50	M	18	H
Environmental scientists and geoscientists			•	•	•					•		•		44	H	21	H
Physicists/astronomers			•	•										83	M	1.1	H
Life Scientists																	
Agricultural/food scientists			•	•										52	L	1.5	H
Biological/medical scientists			•	•										49	M	30	H
Conservation scientists/ foresters		•	•	•	•			•	•	•				47	L	2.2	H

OCCUPATION	JOB REQUIREMENTS								WORK ENVIRONMENT				OCCUPATIONAL CHARACTERISTICS				
	1*	2*	3*	4	5*	6*	7*	8*	9*	10*	11*	12*	13*	14*	15*	16*	17*
Social Scientists/Urban Planners																	
Economists			•	•										65	H	34	H
Psychologists		•	•	•		•								49	M	33	H
Sociologists			•	•		•								46	M	2.6	H
Urban/regional planners	•		•	•	•	•								47	M	4.9	H
Social workers	•	•	•	•	•	•								31	H	141	H
Health-Diagnosing/Treatment Practitioners																	
Chiropractors	•	•	•	•	•	•	•							67	H	12	H
Dentists	•	•	•	•	•	•	•	•						129	L	8.8	H
Optometrists	•	•	•	•	•	•	•	•						83	M	5.9	H
Physicians/surgeons	•	•	•	•	•	•	•	•						160	M	107	H
Podiatrists	•	•	•	•	•	•	•	•						108	M	2.5	H
Veterinarians	•	•	•	•	•	•	•	•						61	H	19	H
Registered Nurses/Pharmacists/Dietitians/Therapists/Physician Assistants																	
Dietitians/nutritionists	•	•	•	•	•	•								38	M	7.4	H
Occupational therapists	•	•	•	•	•	•	•	•						49	H	27	H
Pharmacists	•	•	•	•	•	•					•			71	H	53	H
Physical therapists	•	•	•	•	•	•	•	•						55	H	44	H
Physician assistants	•	•	•	•	•	•	•							62	H	31	H
Recreational therapists	•	•	•	•	•	•	•	•		•				29	L	2.5	H

*1. Leadership/persuasion
*2. Helping/instructing others
*3. Problem solving/creativity
*4. Initiative
*5. Working as part of a team
*6. Frequent public contact
*7. Manual dexterity
*8. Physical stamina

*9. Hazardous
*10. Outdoors
*11. Confined
*12. Geographically concentrated
*13. Part-time
*14. Median annual earnings, 2000 (in thousands)
*15. Employment growth

*16. Number of new jobs, 2000–2010 (in thousands)
*17. Entry requirements (cols.15 & 17):
H = hard
M = medium
L = low
D = decline

Continued

Table 2.1 *Continued*

OCCUPATION	JOB REQUIREMENTS								WORK ENVIRONMENT				OCCUPATIONAL CHARACTERISTICS			
	1*	2*	3*	4	5*	6*	7*	8*	9*	10*	11*	12*	13*	14*	15*	16*	17*
Registered Nurses/Pharmacists/Dietitians/Therapists/Physician Assistants, *continued*																	
Registered nurses	•	•	•	•	•	•	•	•	•				•	45	H	561	M
Respiratory therapists	•	•	•	•	•	•	•							38	M	38	M
Speech-language pathologists/ audiologists	•	•	•	•	•	•								47	M	40	H
Health Technologists/Technicians																	
Cardiovascular technologists/technicians		•	•		•	•	•							33	H	14	M
Cllinical laboratory technologists/technicians		•			•		•				•			41	M	53	H
Dental hygienists		•			•	•	•	•					•	48	H	54	M
Dental laboratory technicians							•				•			26	L	2.7	M
Diagnostic medical sonographers		•	•		•	•	•							45	H	8.6	M
Dispensing opticians		•	•	•	•	•	•							24	M	13	M
Emergency medical technicians/paramedics	•	•	•	•	•	•	•	•	•	•				22	H	54	M
Licensed practical nurses		•			•	•	•	•	•					29	M	142	M
Medical records/health information technicians					•	•					•			23	H	66	M
Nuclear medicine technologists		•			•	•	•							44	H	4.1	M
Occupational health and safety specialists/technicians		•	•	•	•	•		•	•	•				43	M	5.2	H
Pharmacy technicians					•	•					•			20	H	69	M
Radiological technologists/ technicians		•			•	•	•		•					29	H	39	M
Surgical technologists		•			•	•	•							29	H	25	M

OCCUPATION	JOB REQUIREMENTS								WORK ENVIRONMENT				OCCUPATIONAL CHARACTERISTICS				
	1*	2*	3*	4	5*	6*	7*	8*	9*	10*	11*	12*	13*	14*	15*	16*	17*
Health Service Occupations																	
Dental assistants		•			•	•	•	•					•	25	H	92	M
Medical assistants		•			•	•	•		•					23	H	187	M
Nursing/psychiatric/ home health aides		•			•	•	•	•	•				•	20	H	623	L
Occupational/physical therapy assistants/aides		•			•	•	•	•	•					34	H	10	M
Educational/Administrative Occupations																	
College/university faculty	•	•	•	•	•	•		•					•	46	H	315	H
Engineering/natural sciences managers														84	L	26	H
Medical/health services managers	•	•	•	•	•	•								56	H	81	H
Engineering/Science Technicians																	
Cartographers/ photogrammetrists					•		•				•			39	M	NA	H
Drafters					•		•				•			36	M	42	M
Engineering technicians			•		•		•							40	M	62	M
Science technicians			•		•		•							17	M	34	M
Surveying technicians	•		•	•	•		•	•		•				27	M	NA	M

*1. Leadership/persuasion
*2. Helping/instructing others
*3. Problem solving/creativity
*4. Initiative
*5. Working as part of a team
*6. Frequent public contact
*7. Manual dexterity
*8. Physical stamina

*9. Hazardous
*10. Outdoors
*11. Confined
*12. Geographically concentrated
*13. Part-time
*14. Median annual earnings, 2000 (in thousands)

*15. Employment growth
*16. Number of new jobs, 2000–2010 (in thousands)
*17. Entry requirements (cols.15 & 17):
 H = hard
 M = medium
 L = low

NA: Estimates not availlable

GETTING THERE

How can you become a scientist? The answer is the same as the answer to any other question of becoming. The process is neither quick nor simple. You work to acquire the skills and knowledge appropriate to your chosen career. And it takes years.

We tend to think of scientists as people who have displayed the research talent, scholarly creativity, and patience required to earn doctoral degrees. This is true enough for teachers on college and university campuses and for researchers on campus and in industry and government laboratories. But it is hardly a complete picture. A great many people who can call themselves scientific workers do not have doctorates. Lab technicians and many health workers may have no more than a two-year (associate) or four-year (bachelor's) college degree. High school science teachers and many engineers may have a bachelor's or master's degree. Teachers at two-year colleges may have only a master's degree or the non-research-oriented doctor of arts (D.A.).

Some scientific workers have no degrees at all. They have acquired their skills and knowledge through on-the-job experience, perhaps in the military, and they are just as qualified as their degreed colleagues. They may actually be more qualified; often, during the time others have spent in a classroom, they have been developing a deep and intimate practical acquaintance with their subject. They can be engineers, naturalists, archaeologists, fossil-hunting paleontologists, geologists, foresters, and more.

It is thus one of the sadder facts of life that many employers insist on degrees as proof of qualification. They also ask for experience, for that does demonstrate fitness for a job, but they rarely settle for experience alone. Therefore, your best path to your chosen career will include both the academic degree and experience. The experience may come in the form of summer or part-time work, by assisting a professor's research, or by working a few years between high school and college or between college and graduate school. The experience will help not only in landing a job but also in providing a better grasp on the more academic classroom learning.

It is worth stressing that people who earn college and graduate degrees also earn higher incomes later in life. A recent study of the Massachusetts labor force by Ralph Whitehead Jr. and Robert J. Lacey found that in 2000 this effect was especially marked among "knowledge workers" (including those in information technology and health care). College-educated knowledge workers earned almost $14,000 more than college-educated workers in other areas.

Table 3.1 shows some of the many possible educational pathways. You can go directly from high school to a doctorate, though many people pause to work a while between the stages of their education. We can think of these stages as educational levels, and we can use these levels to characterize various careers. Level 1 careers, such as lab technicians, need at least two years of college. Level 2 careers need four years of college. Level 3 careers need a master's degree. Level 4 careers call for at least a doctorate.

A high school graduate can enter the job market directly or go on for a two- or four-year degree. A college graduate can get a job or another degree. You can pause between any two stages of your education to work, or you can go all the way to a doctorate before starting the working phase of your career.

People can of course obtain more than one master's degree or doctorate. A medical researcher may need both a Ph.D. and an M.D. A patent lawyer may need both a law degree and a master's or doctorate in science or engineering. A manager may need to add an M.B.A. to his or her science or engineering degree. Rare individuals may acquire several master's or doctorate degrees; some almost seem to have chosen careers as perpetual students.

Table 3.1 Educational Pathways

TYPE OF WORK	EDUCATION	LEVEL
Transitional, dead-end jobs	High school	0
Lab technicians, paramedics, nurses, allied health workers	Two-year college (community college and vocational school)	1
High school teachers, lab technicians, allied health workers, engineers, foresters	Four-year college	2
High school and two-year and four-year college teachers, research associates, foresters, engineers	Graduate school, master's degree	3
College and university teachers, industry and government researchers and managers, physicians, dentists	Graduate school, doctorate (Ph.D., D.A., D.Sc.); professional schools (medical, dental, veterinary, law)	4

Note that in pursuing a career, more than one graduate degree can be acquired at levels 3 and 4.

LEVEL 0: HIGH SCHOOL PREPARATION

Those who are considering a career in science, no matter how much education they hope to acquire, should begin their preparation in high school. They should take every science course available—biology, chemistry, physics, and more if possible. These courses will provide a first real taste of science and a first exposure to the various fields of science. They will provide a first chance to discover whether science really appeals and a first, light sampling of the available specialties.

In addition, the would-be scientist should take all the mathematics courses available, up to and beyond calculus, for mathematics is often called "the language of science." As many courses as possible in computers and computer programming will also prove very useful, since there is virtually no branch of modern science that does not use computers extensively.

A good knowledge of the English language is also essential, for the scientist must be able to communicate clearly, concisely, and precisely. Scientists must be able to say what they mean without confusion and in as few words as possible. Unfortunately, many scientists fail on this count. Too much scientific prose is wordy, murky, jargon laden, and confusing. It slows reading and learning, aggravates journal editors, and worsens the writer's chances of communicating and of being promoted.

Bear in mind that everyone appreciates a good speaker and writer. All students—not just would-be scientists—should thus take plenty of English courses and practice their composition. They should read all they can, pay attention to how writers write, and try to match what they read in their own efforts. As they become better writers, they will be pleased to find how much easier writing becomes.

Foreign languages are very useful. Most graduate schools once required a reading knowledge of two foreign languages. Most now ask for no more than one; if a second is required, it may be a computer programming language such as C++ or JAVA. The one human language should be a language that will make it easier for the student to read widely in his or her field, one in which reports and papers are published. Once this meant German, since most non-English-language research was once done in Germany. Now it could be German, French, Spanish, Russian, Japanese, or Chinese. German, French, and Spanish are offered in many high schools. Russian, Japanese, and Chinese should be offered, for they are now the more useful to many scientists.

Fortunately, a great deal of foreign research is published in English, and most of the scientists who meet at international scientific meetings speak English as a second language. However, the ability to read and even speak some language other than English is invaluable for more than simply satisfying academic requirements. Its professional benefit is speedier, more effective communication. Many people believe it is also valuable for the way it opens another culture—its music, literature, and history—to the person who speaks or reads its tongue. Whatever their reason, students should begin acquiring other languages early in their education. Later, they will need the time languages demand for study in their specialties.

High school students should not neglect their other courses, for scientists are as much a part of the world as anyone else and must know as much about it. Still, if they do concentrate on their professional preparation, they will also be well prepared to switch if necessary to another field, even to a nonscience such as history or politics. Preparation for science, because it is so broad and inclusive and because it inculcates the habits of a logical, orderly mind, is preparation for almost anything. Those who have trouble making up their mind in high school may do well to bear this in mind and to remember that few college students have chosen their career before their junior year. Some are still undecided after graduate school.

LEVEL 1: THE TWO-YEAR EDUCATION

Many high school graduates who want to pursue their education do not go directly to a four-year college or university. They may not be able to afford the high tuition. They may not qualify for various financial aid programs, and they may not wish to take out loans to cover the costs of four years of full-time schooling.

Perhaps they are just plain sick of school or uncertain of their career direction. They want to work for a year or two to gather experience, sample possibilities, and save money for later schooling. When they do return to school, they may do so tentatively, attending classes part-time or in the evening. They may very well look for a less expensive school or seek education that prepares them quickly and specifically for better jobs. They may have no patience for the smorgasbord approach that helps so many college students find their careers. They may want education that is more tailored to the interests they develop as they work.

Professional schools fill this need for college graduates. There are also numerous four-year technical schools. But what is there for students with lower immediate aspirations and slimmer purses?

The extension ("continuing education") courses offered by state universities have traditionally met these students' needs. Now there are also many junior or community colleges that offer two-year associate of arts (A.A.) or associate of science (A.S.) degrees, often with a very vocational emphasis. There are two-year programs for lab technicians in biology and other sciences and for allied health workers. There are also two-year technical and vocational institutes, trade schools, and formal and informal apprenticeship programs.

According to the National Science Foundation, the number of science and engineering associate degrees awarded each year varies from 50,000 to 60,000, with about half awarded in the computer sciences. Engineering technicians alone earned 33,000 associate degrees in 1997.

The great virtue of these programs is that they offer a slower, less intensive, and less expensive approach to higher education. They also prepare their students to transfer to a four-year school to obtain a bachelor's degree in two more years, while also offering a natural stopping point after the A.A. or A.S. They do not offer a lower-quality education, although two-year schools, like four-year schools, do vary in quality. They do offer a briefer, and hence less extensive, education. For many students, they are a first step. For some, they are enough, for they do prepare students adequately for many careers.

The greatest drawback to a two-year education may be its lack of breadth. The four-year liberal arts education, which cultivates not specific job skills but the ability to think and live well in the world, impresses many as producing a well-rounded, even an ideal, human being. But the "school of hard knocks" can have a very similar effect.

LEVEL 2: THE FOUR-YEAR EDUCATION

The four-year schools are colleges and universities. The educations they offer vary greatly in quality but less in kind. These schools generally follow one of two approaches to educating their students. The first is the liberal arts approach. It encourages students to take a wide variety of courses, both to broaden their minds and to expose them to many possible career directions. In their second or third year of college, students choose a "major" field, in which they then concentrate their studies. This approach is common in small colleges.

The second, professional approach appears more often in technical schools and institutes and in large universities. Students may enroll in a university's school of forestry or engineering or business and choose a major within that narrow field. In a school of arts and sciences, they may also find a more liberal education, with majors in English, biology, or anthropology. Often, students begin broadly in arts and sciences and later move into a field-oriented school. Note that Table 3.2, which tallies the number of science and engineering bachelor's degrees awarded, does not distinguish between the liberal arts and professional approaches.

Table 3.2 Earned Bachelor's Degrees, by Field, 1975–1998 (Selected Years)

FIELD	1975	1985	1995	1998
Total all fields	**931,663**	**990,877**	**1,174,436**	**1,199,579**
Total science and engineering	**313,555**	**332,273**	**378,148**	**390,618**
Natural sciences	87,199	75,158	90,845	104,673
Biological and agricultural sciences	66,321	51,312	71,470	85,079
Earth/atmospheric/ocean sciences	4,877	7,576	4,478	4,321
Physical sciences	16,001	16,270	14,897	15,273
Mathematics and computer sciences	23,385	54,510	38,620	39,768
Computer sciences	5,039	39,121	24,769	27,674
Mathematics	18,346	15,389	13,851	12,094
Social and behavioral sciences	163,147	125,033	185,312	185,263
Psychology	51,436	40,237	72,601	74,457
Social sciences	111,711	84,796	112,711	110,806
Engineering	39,824	77,572	63,371	60,914
Chemical	3,420	8,941	6,391	6,721
Civil	8,289	9,730	11,329	11,522
Electrical	10,246	23,668	17,579	16,322
Industrial	2,583	4,009	3,519	3,988
Mechanical	7,089	17,200	15,141	13,363
Other	8,197	14,024	9,412	8,998
Engineering technologies	8,589	20,476	16,607	14,825

Source: National Science Board, *Science and Engineering Indicators, 2002,* (Arlington, VA: National Science Foundation, 2002) NSB-02-1.

The professional approach often gives students specific job skills. It equips them to step into a job immediately. The liberal arts approach transmits a body of more general knowledge. Often, its avowed aim is to teach habits of thought and study. It thus equips students less for jobs than for further education, perhaps in graduate school or in the form of on-the-job training.

Each field of science has its own body of knowledge, and the college student begins to acquire that knowledge with an introductory survey course. Later courses cover specialties within the field in greater depth. For instance, a college freshman who wants to major in chemistry will take "freshman chem" for an overview of the field of chemistry and its basic principles. Later, he or she will take organic chemistry, biochemistry, and physical chemistry. Larger schools may also offer courses in quantum chemistry, catalysis, and spectroscopy.

In all the sciences (except mathematics and some social sciences), most courses are accompanied by a laboratory. Here, students learn the techniques of the field and specialty they are studying. They may even learn techniques that amount to job skills, although many schools do not have laboratory equipment as up-to-date as the working labs of industry and government. Students often learn the skills of a past generation of scientists and must depend on their knowledge of methods and principles to help them catch on quickly once they are out of school. They usually succeed, but many scientific educators are deeply concerned with this disparity between education and practice. They yearn for industry, government, and foundation funding to buy modern equipment. Government has affirmed the value of science and education and expressed its own concern over outdated laboratory equipment, though funding is in short supply. Students must thus depend on part-time and summer jobs to bring their technical skills up to current standards or else must rush to catch up once they have their first career position.

Science students should take all the courses and labs within their major field for which they have the time. But they should also do more. They should take English courses to boost their communication skills, both written and oral. They should become proficient with computers. They must study math and statistics, a requirement that cannot be too strongly emphasized. Statistics is essential in the designing of experiments and for the analysis of data in every field. Math is equally essential to understanding and building explanatory models or theories, and while all the sciences use calculus and differential equations, some use abstract algebras, tensor calculus, fiber bundles, and other mathematical esoterica.

Science students should also take science courses outside their field. Biologists and astronomers invariably need at least a good grounding in chemistry and physics. Engineers and geologists need biology, chemistry, and physics. Chemists need physics. Physicists need chemistry. All can benefit from taking at least the survey courses in each of the other fields.

There are limits, however. In a small school, students can hope to take every available course in their major field and the survey courses for every other science represented on campus. At a large university, they may not have the time to take even half the courses in their major, and they may have to pick and choose very carefully to find the survey courses most pertinent to their major. Moreover, the large university may demand more specialization at the bachelor's level; the student will major in zoology or biochemistry or solid-state physics instead of biology, chemistry, or physics. Nevertheless, the student should gain as broad a scientific education as possible. It will not be wasted. It may even prove invaluable, for the greatest discoveries are often made by people who can combine the concepts or data of two or more fields.

Many students approach college having already chosen a major field, and they look for a school with a top reputation in that field. If that school does not accept them, they feel like failures before they have even begun their careers. Yet it is not only the biggest schools with the most varied offerings and the most glittering reputations that are worth attending. Small, relatively unknown schools can often offer excellent preparation for a career in science, and many outstanding scientists have come from small colleges best known only within a single state or region. The small liberal arts schools have, for instance, graduated a number of top biologists all out of proportion to their collective size. The best way to judge a school, if it offers the necessary basic courses, may be to ask whether its graduates have been able to enroll in top graduate schools or to win choice positions in industry and government.

Every student in every school will benefit tremendously from actual experience in his or her specialty. This experience can take the form of serving as a teaching assistant in lab courses, a job often open to undergraduate seniors. It can mean helping a faculty member in research. It can mean part-time or summer jobs off campus working in industry, research labs, museums, parks, or zoos. Such experience provides a taste of the future and a basis for changing one's mind. It may also introduce a student to research interests that will prove absorbing throughout a long career. In addition, it can help pay the costs of a college education.

LEVEL 3: THE MASTER'S DEGREE

It is apparent from a cursory comparison of Tables 3.2 and 3.3 that about a quarter of all science and engineering bachelor's graduates go on to earn a master's degree in their original field or a related field. Those who do pursue

Table 3.3 Earned Master's Degrees, by Field: 1977–1998 (Selected Years)

FIELD	1977	1987	1997	1998
Total all fields	**293,651**	**290,931**	**420,954**	**431,871**
Total science and engineering	**63,198**	**67,733**	**93,485**	**93,918**
Natural sciences	14,831	14,380	16,097	15,625
Biological and agricultural sciences	9,030	9,136	10,521	10,230
Earth/atmospheric/ocean sciences	1,503	1,959	1,435	1,426
Physical sciences	4,298	3,285	4,141	3,969
Mathematics and computer sciences	6,637	8,177	14,088	15,277
Computer sciences	2,299	5,321	10,489	11,752
Mathematics	4,338	2,856	3,599	3,525
Social and behavioral sciences	26,563	26,290	37,426	36,878
Psychology	7,104	8,439	13,633	13,146
Social sciences	19,459	17,851	23,793	23,732
Engineering	15,167	18,886	25,874	26,138
Chemical	1,078	1,545	1,345	1,372
Civil	3,268	3,504	4,880	4,736
Electrical	3,471	4,819	7,341	7,971
Industrial	1,687	1,432	2,935	3,109
Mechanical	2,032	2,683	3,756	3,551
Other	3,631	4,903	5,617	5,399
Engineering technologies	371	622	1,414	1,700

Source: National Science Board, *Science and Engineering Indicators, 2002 (*Arlington, VA: National Science Foundation, 2002) NSB-02-1.

the master's degree spend one or two more years in school, taking more specialized courses than they could find in college and acquiring skills more closely related to what they will need on the job. They do not usually get involved in their own original research. The thesis often required for the master's degree depends more on the library than on the laboratory. Its function is to demonstrate command of a body of knowledge.

Many people set a master's degree as their goal. The degree is the one they need for the career they have in mind. They have no interest in original research. They do not, at this point in their lives, plan to become researchers or professors. And their needs are met by most graduate schools.

However, some schools—or some departments within many schools—do not offer the master's degree as an end in itself. They see it as a way station, a certificate that says one has made a certain amount of progress toward a doctorate. Students may choose to stop their studies at this point either because they have run out of patience (or funds) or because they have found the limits of their ability.

LEVEL 4: THE DOCTORATE

Different fields of science and engineering produce different numbers of doctoral graduates (see Table 3.4). Interestingly, fields that produce the greatest number of doctorates (such as the social sciences) may see only a small portion of their bachelor's graduates go on to get the doctorate. In some fields that produce a relatively small number of doctoral graduates, that number is a quarter of the field's bachelor's graduates (see Table 3.5). The percentage of bachelor's graduates that go on to get doctorates is lowest

Table 3.4 Earned Doctoral Degrees by Field: 1975–1999 (Selected Years)

FIELD	1975	1985	1995	1999
Total all fields	**32,952**	**31,297**	**41,743**	**41,140**
Total science and engineering	**18,799**	**18,935**	**26,535**	**25,953**
Natural sciences	8,103	8,436	11,024	10,954
Biological and agricultural sciences	4,402	4,903	6,412	6,565
Earth/atmospheric/ocean sciences	625	599	780	807
Physical sciences	3,076	2,934	3,841	3,582
Mathematics and computer sciences	1,360	998	2,187	1,935
Mathematics	1,147	688	1,190	1,085
Computer sciences	213	310	997	850
Social and behavioral sciences	6,538	6,335	7,307	7,727
Psychology	2,751	3,118	3,429	3,667
Social sciences	3,787	3,217	3,878	4,060
Engineering	3,011	3,166	6,008	5,337
Chemical	396	504	708	678
Civil	361	391	656	585
Electrical	714	716	1,731	1,477
Mechanical	487	513	1,025	853
Materials	272	303	588	470
Other	781	739	1,300	1,274

Source: National Science Board, *Science and Engineering Indicators, 2002* (Arlington, VA: National Science Foundation, 2002) NSB-02-1.

Table 3.5 Earned Doctoral Degrees as Percentage of Earned Bachelor's Degrees, 1998

FIELD	BACHELORS	DOCTORATES	PERCENT
Total all fields	**1,199,579**	**42,683**	**3.56%**
Total science and engineering	**390,618**	**27,309**	**6.99%**
Natural sciences	104,673	11,534	11.02%
Biological and agricultural sciences	85,079	6,891	8.10%
Earth/atmospheric/ocean sciences	4,321	814	18.84%
Physical sciences	15,273	3,829	25.07%
Mathematics and computer sciences	39,768	2,102	5.29%
Mathematics	12,094	1,177	9.73%
Computer sciences	27,674	925	3.34%
Social and behavioral sciences	185,263	7,743	4.18%
Psychology	74,457	3,685	4.95%
Social sciences	110,806	4,058	3.66%
Engineering	60,914	5,930	9.74%
Chemical	6,721	775	11.53%
Civil	11,522	651	5.65%
Electrical	16,322	1,596	9.78%
Industrial	3,988	1,023	25.65%
Mechanical	13,363	565	4.23%
Other	8,998	1,320	14.67%

Source: National Science Board, *Science and Engineering Indicators, 2002* (Arlington, VA: National Science Foundation, 2002) NSB-02-1.

in mathematics, computer science, and the social sciences, where the demand is highest for people in bachelor-level jobs. In computer science, bachelor's graduates can receive pay so high that they have little incentive to stay in school. The percentage of doctorates is highest in the physical sciences (physics and chemistry) and industrial engineering, which employ many researchers.

The doctorate marks the highest level of educational achievement in this country. The first U.S. Ph.D. (doctor of philosophy) program was set up by Yale University in 1860, and the Ph.D. is now the degree of the skilled teacher, scholar, and researcher. The requirements for the Ph.D. may vary from school to school and from field to field, but they always include the fact of specialization. It is in graduate school that biologists become ichthyologists and geneticists, that physicists specialize in optics and particle theory, that chemists focus on catalysts and spectroscopy. In the process, they satisfy foreign language requirements, pass an intensive exam on their knowledge of their specialty (and perhaps collect a way station master's), select an original research topic, do the research, write a thesis or dissertation presenting the results of that research, and defend the thesis or dissertation orally before a faculty committee. The object of their ordeal—which can last five or more years—is to ensure that they know their field and are capable of original contributions to it. Along the way, they may assist in teaching and research, learning the practical skills they will need and helping to pay their educational and personal bills.

There are alternatives to the Ph.D. at the doctoral level. The D.Sc. (doctor of science) is an equivalent degree offered by some schools to students who are planning a career in research. The D.A. (doctor of arts) is for those who plan to make a career of teaching, with little or no research; it emphasizes preparation for teaching. The M.D. (doctor of medicine) is for those interested in the healing applications of science, especially of biology. Medical schools offer both classroom learning and clinical experience in a hospital. Other specialized professional schools train veterinarians, dentists, optometrists, and osteopaths, and they offer their own degrees.

In the case of medicine, further specialization may follow medical school and the M.D. There is some room for specialization within a medical program, but neurologists, proctologists, cardiac surgeons, and other specialists gain many of their unique skills in later internships and residencies, working in hospitals under more experienced experts. Their postgraduate training is a combination of seminars and hands-on apprenticeship. Even with no time out for work experience, physicians may thus not be fully trained until they are in their thirties.

Students facing four years of college and up to five (or more) years of graduate training often find the prospect a depressingly long grind. Yet every career requires a long apprenticeship and years of training and skill building. The high school, community college, or college graduate who begins his or her working career immediately, without further academic schooling, must spend those years on the job. The big difference is that the job pays, while school costs, although on-the-job training produces no paper certification of education or competence.

The long apprenticeship is just as necessary for musicians, writers, artists, businesspeople, and politicians as it is for scientists. Doctoral-level scientists emerge from graduate school as young as twenty-six or twenty-seven or, if they take off a few years for work experience, their early thirties. They have a degree that documents their abilities. They may even, in their doctoral research, have already made a valuable contribution to the scientific literature, for it is not at all unusual for graduate students to publish their original work. Graduate students thereby act as fully professional research scientists, including their years in graduate school in their definition of career.

PAYING FOR SCHOOL

The four levels of education beyond high school correspond roughly to four levels of careers. Where a high school graduate cannot become much more than a laboratory gofer ("Go fer this, go fer that"), a stockroom clerk, a veterinary attendant, or a trainee technician, the worker with a two-year degree can be a trained lab technician, an allied health worker, or an engineering aide. The four-year college graduate can be an engineer, forester, medical technician, or high school teacher. A master's degree opens up the field of college teaching, provides entrée to scientific research, and lets the degree holder attain higher levels as a technician or engineer. A doctorate lets one join the faculties of major schools, take charge of research, or practice medicine.

Each of these four levels of education and career is attainable. All the beginner needs is interest, intelligence, and a willingness to work hard. Patience and determination help. The motivation can be curiosity, ambition, or simple greed, for at each level one's income does go up.

The biggest obstacle may be the expense of education. According to the College Board, in 1998–99, students attending public colleges and universities paid an average tuition bill of $10,458. Students at private colleges and universities paid an average of $22,533 for that year. Room, board, texts, and other expenses may run the student's budget to well over $30,000 a year. To make things worse, tuition expenses are rising at 5 to 6 percent per year. Some students can tap their family for the funds they need, at least as undergraduates. Other students must find their funds themselves.

Fortunately, it is possible to find the necessary money. Part-time and summer jobs help. Some students work full time and take courses as they can afford them. Many employers will pay tuition and allow time off for employee studies. Some will pay for a student's education in return for a promise that the student will work for them for a certain number of years after graduation. In cooperative education, the student alternates periods of on-campus schooling with paid on-the-job experience. Internships place advanced undergraduate and graduate students who have already gained a fair amount of competence in their field in part-time professional settings and can involve pay; more often they are for academic credit only.

There are also scholarships and grants available to those who qualify for them. Some are small and some large. Many schools have their own, representing donations intended to help, for instance, "left-handed Congregationalist orphans" (the example is only half facetious). Others come from such outside sources as the Daughters of the American Revolution, churches, foundations, and the National Merit program (www.nationalmerit.org). College catalogs are useful sources of information. So are state educational agencies. A compilation of books and websites is provided at the end of this chapter; current editions of the books should be available in your high school guidance office or library.

There are also loans. Of most interest are those with low-interest rates and repayment guaranteed by the government. Guidance counselors and college financial assistance offices have the necessary information. Some loans need no repayment at all if, after graduation, the student works in a specific place for a specific employer for a few years. Medical students may pay their way by agreeing to work in out-of-the-way areas. The money may come from the federal government, a state, or even, occasionally, a town that desperately needs a doctor. One recent source of such loans is the Cyber Corps, or Federal Cyber Service: Scholarship for Service program; the federal government, through the National Science Foundation, pays the tuition (and expenses) for two years for computer science students studying computer security. In return, the students work for the government for two years.

The Federal Student Guide (ed.gov/prog_info/SFA/StudentGuide/ 2002–3/ index.html) describes five major student financial aid programs offered by the U.S. Department of Education, along with the necessary application information. These programs account for about 70 percent of all college financial aid. To obtain federal aid, students must fill out and submit the Free Application for Federal Student Aid (FAFSA).

Federal student aid is financial help for students enrolled in eligible programs at participating schools to cover school (a four-year or two-year public or private educational institution, a career school or trade school) expenses, including tuition and fees, room and board, books and supplies, and transportation. Most federal aid is need-based. The three most common types of aid are grants, loans, and work-study.

Grants

Financial aid that does not have to be repaid is a grant. Generally, grants are for undergraduate students, and the grant amount is based on need, cost of attendance, and enrollment status.

Federal Pell Grants for the 2002–2003 school year range from $400 to $4,000.

Federal Supplemental Educational Opportunity Grants (FSEOG) range from $100 to $4,000.

Loans

Borrowed money that must be repaid with interest is a loan. Both undergraduate and graduate students may borrow money. Parents may also borrow to pay education expenses for dependent undergraduate students. Maximum loan amounts depend on the student's year in school.

Federal Stafford Loans are made to students and PLUS loans are made to parents through two loan programs:

1. William D. Ford Federal Direct Loan (Direct Loan) Program: eligible students and parents borrow directly from the federal government and participating schools. Direct Loans include Direct Stafford Loans, Direct PLUS Loans, and Direct Consolidation Loans.
2. Federal Family Education Loan (FFEL) Program: private lenders provide federally guaranteed funds. FFELs include FFEL Stafford Loans, FFEL PLUS Loans, and FFEL Consolidation Loans.

Perkins Loans are offered by participating schools to provide students that demonstrate the most need with low-interest loans.

Work-Study

Work-study lets you earn money while enrolled in school to help pay for education expenses.

The guaranteed loans (including PLUS and Stafford loans) are low-interest loans made to students and parents by financial institutions, such as banks, and are insured (guaranteed) by state and federal agencies. Repayment begins six months after the student graduates or leaves school and may take five to ten years. PLUS loans permit parents to borrow up to the estimated cost of school (less financial aid) each year. Stafford loans permit dependent students to borrow up to $2,625 for the first undergraduate academic year, $3,500 for the second, and $5,500 for the third and fourth. Nondependent undergraduates may borrow up to $6,625, $7,500, and $10,500. Graduate students may borrow up to $18,500 per year.

Something to bear in mind is that very few students pay all their college expenses—or even most of them—with loans. Even low-income students (or their families) tend to cover less than half the bill with loans. The rest is covered by need-based grants, scholarships, work-study programs, and part-time and summer jobs.

How do students find financial aid? There are a great many books and websites designed to help (see sources at the end of this chapter), but every college has a financial aid office designed to help. Typically, the financial aid process begins with a "needs analysis" that takes into account the student's family's current income, number of children in college, expenses, and assets and sets an "expected contribution" of the family toward the student's expenses. Because this figure is often considerably less than the student's expenses, the school then offers scholarships and part-time (federally supported work-study) jobs on campus to help. The school also administers federal Pell Grants, Supplemental Educational Opportunity Grants, and Perkins, PLUS, and Stafford loans (explained earlier).

Most American families fall somewhere between rich and poor—neither rich enough to pay for a complete college education out of pocket nor poor enough to get a complete scholarship. In such cases, the expected family contribution (from savings, a second mortgage, and/or a PLUS loan) to the first-year expenses might cover a tenth of the first-year bill. The student will be expected to provide as much or more from summer work and savings. A scholarship might stretch to half the total, with Perkins and Stafford loans and a work-study assignment covering the rest.

Many people recommend that college freshmen not try to both work and study. College is a very different place from high school. The student must adjust to a new social and physical environment, to a heavier workload, and to new study habits. While this adjustment is still going on, students should not—if possible—make things harder for themselves by taking on extra work. Unfortunately, this means that college students should have their first year's expenses in hand at the start. This may be difficult, if not impossible, and the situation does not seem likely to improve. Costs do keep going up.

Graduate school is less of a financial problem. Many schools will go to great lengths to help promising students complete their studies. They have teaching and research assistantships, which pay a stipend and tuition. They have access to government training grants, industry and foundation money, and other sources, and they use these funds to keep the best students. This means that good students need not worry, but it also means that many graduate school classes are taught by older students. The nominal professors may rarely emerge from their labs, preferring to let their teaching assistants handle what they themselves see as a chore. This needn't be all bad, however. Some researchers are stimulating lecturers, but some are not. Their assistants may actually be much better teachers.

The professional schools are less helpful. There are scholarships, but more often students must borrow the money they need. Financial assistance for medical school (to take one type of professional school as an example) can come from a diverse array of loans and scholarships. Loans can come from banks, the Health Professions Student Loan Program (see http://bhpr.hrsa.gov/dsa/pages/programs.htm), or the Department of Education's Guaranteed Student Loan Program (Stafford and Perkins loans are also available for graduate study). Scholarships can come from the schools, the National Science Foundation, the Defense Department's Armed Forces Health Professions Scholarship Program (see http://nshs.med.navy.mil /hpsp/Pages/HPSPHome.htm; funds to be repaid by service as a commissioned officer), or the National Health Service Corps Scholarship Program (see http://www.cfda.gov/public/viewprog.asp?progid=1238; funds to be repaid by working for at least two years in a "health manpower-shortage area"). Most medical schools discourage part-time work, as medical study is very demanding.

Not every student qualifies for scholarships or grants. Loans are much easier to get, even though students may balk at the thought of putting themselves tens of thousands of dollars in debt for years to come. Perhaps it will help if we try to put these loans in perspective. Public medical schools may charge tuition under $20,000 per year. Private schools may have tuitions approaching $60,000. Expenses inflate the bill further. To become a physician, a student will take courses for three years and then spend three to eight years as a low-paid resident. A medical student may thus owe well over $200,000 by the time he or she is a practicing physician. This is certainly a forbidding sum, but a young physician can easily make over $100,000 a year (in 1998, the median net income of physicians, after expenses, was $160,000); if he or she is a specialist in an urban area, that sum can double or triple. It seems little trouble for the physician to repay the $200,000 within a few years. Even counting the interest on the loan, the physician will still have plenty of money left to support a comfortable lifestyle.

A bachelor's, master's, or Ph.D. graduate cannot expect to earn a physician's pay, but then he or she won't need to borrow as much money either. At the same time, the degree will increase the graduate's income enough to make repaying the loan relatively painless. This is especially true in fields such as engineering and computer science.

Sources of Financial Aid Information

Barry Beckham, ed., *The Black Student's Guide to Scholarships: 700+ Private Money Sources for Black and Minority Students*, 5th ed. New York: Madison Books, 1999.

The College Cost and Financial Aid Handbook 2003. New York: The College Entrance Examination Board, 2002.

R. David Weber and Gail A. Schlachter, *College Student's Guide to Merit and Other No-Need Funding, 2002–2004*. El Dorado Hills, CA: Reference Service Press, 2002.

Gail Schlachter, *Directory of Financial Aid for Women, 2001–2003*. El Dorado Hills, CA: Reference Service Press, 2001.

Gail Schlachter, R. David Weber, and Douglas Bucher, *Kaplan Scholarships 2003*. New York: Kaplan, 2002.

Gail A. Schlachter and R. David Weber, *Financial Aid for African Americans, 2001–2003*. El Dorado Hills, CA: Reference Service Press, 2001.

Gail A. Schlachter and R. David Weber, *Financial Aid for Asian Americans, 2001–2003*. El Dorado Hills, CA: Reference Service Press, 2001.

Gail A. Schlachter and R. David Weber, *Financial Aid for Hispanic Americans, 2001–2003*. El Dorado Hills, CA: Reference Service Press, 2001.

Student Financial Services, *The Government Financial Aid Book: The Insider's Guide to State and Federal Government Grants and Loans*, 4th ed. Seattle: Perpetual Press, 2002.

Peterson's Scholarships for Study in the USA and Canada: Get the Money You Need for the Education You Want. Lawrenceville, NJ: Peterson's Guides, 1999.

Chrystal Rozsa and William A. Richards, eds., *Scholarships, Fellowships and Loans: A Guide to Education-Related Financial Aid Programs for Students and Professionals*. Farmington Hills, MI: Gale Group, 2002.

National Scholarship Research Service, *The Scholarship Book 2003: The Complete Guide to Private-Sector Scholarships, Fellowships, Grants and Loans for the Undergraduate*. Upper Saddle River, NJ: Prentice-Hall Press, 2002.

On the Web

The Educational Testing Service's "College Costs—A Field Guide": www.ets.org/fpoints

Fast Web (Financial Aid Search Through the Web): www.fastweb.com

http://Free Application for Federal Student Aid (FAFSA)
    To file online: www.ed.gov/offices/OPE/express.html
    To file by mail: www.ed.gov/prog_info/SFA/FAFSA

2002–2003 Federal Student Guide: www.ed.gov/prog_info/SFA/Student Guide/2002–3/index.html

The SmartStudent Guide to Financial Aid: finaid.org/finaid.html

4

CAREERS IN HELPING AND SOCIAL SCIENCES

By far, the great majority of science careers are related to health. Physicians, nurses, psychologists, opticians, hospital administrators, medical technicians, and many more add up to some 9.6 million people. The other people-related sciences—the social sciences—employ another 360,000 men and women. Social workers add 468,000. All the other sciences combined—the life, earth, space, and physical sciences, engineering, mathematics, and the computer sciences—employ only 6.5 million people.

Most of this book will be devoted to the latter group. The less people-related sciences are, after all, much more what we think of when we think "science," and we are more likely to have them in mind when we think of careers in science. However, careers in health and in social science are careers in science. Furthermore, health careers as a group will grow faster than average as the aging of the American population increases the need for health care. In fact, many health-related careers are among the occupations with the greatest projected growth through 2010.

Careers in health and social science thus deserve at least a little attention here, and thirty-eight careers in the helping (health-related) sciences and four careers in the social sciences are discussed on the following pages. The careers are those listed in the U.S. Department of Labor's *Occupational Outlook Handbook*. Their brief descriptions include necessary education, numbers employed, employment outlook, and pay. Most of the data are as of 2000.

Table 4.1 lists the occupations described in this chapter and summarizes their job prospects through the year 2010 and the educational level they call for (see Chapter 3 for definitions of the levels).

Note that this list does not include some occupations you might be interested in. For example, psychotherapist is not included because psychotherapy is something done by people in several occupations, such as psychiatrists, who are actually physicians. Therapy is also done by clinical and counseling psychologists, clinical social workers, marriage and family counselors or therapists, and clinical mental health counselors. These occupations are covered in more detail later in this chapter.

HELPING SCIENCES

Cardiovascular Technologists

Cardiovascular technologists and *technicians* work with physicians to diagnose and treat cardiovascular ailments. They run the ECG (or EKG) equipment that records the electrical activity of the heart, assist with cardiac catheterization and angioplasty, and run ultrasound scans. Subdivisions include cardiology technologist, cardiographic, electrocardiographic, or EKG technician, cardiovascular technologist, vascular technologist or sonographer, cardiac sonographer, and echocardiographer. There are about 39,000 of them, earning $20,000 to $53,000 a year. Education can be high school plus on-the-job training, but most are graduates of two and four-year academic programs. The job outlook is good, with employment expected to grow faster than the average for all occupations through the year 2010. The outlook is even better for those with more training.

Chiropractors

Chiropractors believe that many human ills lie in misalignments of the body, especially of the spine, which interfere with the functions of the muscular and nervous systems. Some chiropractors specialize in sports injuries. They use X-rays to locate the source of trouble, and they treat with manual adjustment, diet, exercise, and other therapies. State certification requires at least two years of college followed by four years at a chiro-

Table 4.1 Job Prospects in the Helping and Social Sciences, 2000–2010

	PERCENT INCREASE IN EMPLOYMENT	EDUCATIONAL LEVEL REQUIRED
Helping Sciences		
Cardiovascular technologist or technician	35	0, 1, 2
Chiropractor	23	3
Clinical laboratory technologist or technician	18	1, 2
Counselor, rehabilitation	26	3
Dental assistant	37	1
Dental hygienist	37	1, 2
Dental laboratory technician	3	1
Dentist	6	3, 4
Diagnostic medical sonographer	26	1, 2
Dietitian or nutritionist	15	2
Emergency medical technician	31	1
Health services manager	32	2, 3, 4
Licensed practical nurse	20	1
Medical assistant	57	1
Medical record and health information technician	49	1, 2
Nuclear medicine technologist	22	1, 2
Nursing, psychiatric, or home health aide	30	0
Occupational health and safety specialist or technician	15	2
Occupational therapist	34	2
Occupational therapy assistant or aide	42	1
Ophthalmic laboratory technician	5	2
Optician, dispensing	19	1
Optometrist	19	3
Pharmacist	24	2, 3
Pharmacy technician	33	1
Physical therapist	19	2, 3, 4
Physical therapy assistant or aide	45	0, 1
Physician	18	4
Physician assistant	53	1
Podiatrist	14	3, 4
Radiologic technologist or technician	23	1, 2
Recreational therapist	9	1, 2, 3
Registered nurse	26	1, 2
Respiratory therapist	35	1, 2
Social worker	30	2, 3
Speech-language pathologist or audiologist	40	3
Surgical technologist	35	1
Veterinarian	32	3, 4
Social Sciences		
Economist or market or survey researcher	25	2, 3, 4
Psychologist	18	2, 3, 4
Social scientist	16	2, 3, 4
Urban or regional planner	17	3

Source: "Professional and Related" and "Management and Business and Financial Operations,"
Occupational Outlook Quarterly (Spring 2002).

practic college. Median income for salaried chiropractors was $67,030 in 2000; self-employed chiropractors earned an average of $81,500 per year after expenses. There are 50,000 practicing chiropractors in the country, and employment seems likely to grow faster than average through the year 2010 as public acceptance continues to grow.

Clinical Laboratory Technologists/Technicians

The nation's 295,000 *clinical* (or medical) *laboratory technologists* and *technicians* do blood, pathological, immunological, chemical, and other tests in hospital and commercial laboratories. Their work is essential to careful, accurate, thorough diagnosis. Technologists require four years of training; technicians need two years. In 2000, the median annual pay was $40,500, with technologists earning more than technicians. The job outlook is about average.

Rehabilitation Counselors

Rehabilitation counseling is but one specialty within the field of counseling. There are 205,000 educational, vocational, and school counselors, 110,000 rehabilitation counselors, 67,000 mental health counselors, 61,000 substance abuse and behavioral disorder counselors, and 21,000 marriage and family therapists. Rehabilitation counselors help people overcome physical, mental, and emotional handicaps by inventorying talents, skills, and interests and encouraging suitable training. About half of all counselors have master's degrees. *Rehabilitation counselors* averaged $24,450 in 2000, with those working for state governments and hospitals earning $31,000 to $35,000 and those working in residential care earning less than $21,000. Other types of counselors typically do better (educational, vocational, and school counselors averaged $42,000 in 2000). Employment should grow faster than the average for all occupations through the year 2010.

Dental Assistants

Dental assistants prepare materials, pass instruments, take X-rays, and instruct patients in a dentist's office. Many learn their skills on the job;

most graduate from a one- or two-year program at a community or junior college, trade school, or technical institute. The 247,000 employed in this job average annual salaries of about $20,000. The employment outlook through the year 2010 is excellent, with employment expected to grow much faster than average.

Dental Hygienists

The *dental hygienist* takes X-rays, cleans teeth, and instructs patients in proper tooth care. The 147,000 in the field all graduated from accredited dental hygiene schools, most with two-year programs, some with bachelor's or master's programs, and earned state licenses to practice. The job outlook is very good (among the thirty best), and the pay can easily get into the $40,000 to $60,000 ($20- to $30-per-hour) range. However, many jobs in this field are only part-time positions.

Dental Laboratory Technicians

The *dental laboratory technician* makes dentures, crowns, and braces and needs only a high school diploma plus three or four years of on-the-job or apprenticeship training. There are also community college programs. Some 43,000 people hold this job, making about $27,000 per year. The future employment outlook for dental laboratory technicians is poor; the number of jobs is expected to grow very slowly.

Dentists

Dentists clean, repair, and replace teeth; they may also perform surgery on the gums and jaws. The 152,000 practicing dentists have a bachelor's or master's degree plus a two- or four-year dental school degree and average about $129,000 a year. Employment seems likely to grow more slowly than the average for all occupations through the year 2010, but job prospects should remain good because the nation is no longer producing a surplus of dentists and the number of older Americans, who will need a greater amount of dental care, is increasing.

Diagnostic Medical Sonographers

The nation's 33,000 *diagnostic medical sonographers* operate the equipment that provides physicians with images—X-rays, magnetic resonance images (MRI), CAT scans, sonograms, and others—essential for diagnosis and treatment. Training begins with a two- or four-year degree and continues with on-the-job experience. Competency is certified by the American Registry of Diagnostic Medical Sonographers, which sets standards, including a requirement for continuing education. Median pay is $44,820. Employment is expected to grow faster than average through 2010.

Dietitians/Nutritionists

Dietitians and *nutritionists* provide nutritional counseling, run institutional food services, and educate the public. Numbering 49,000, their salaries average $38,450 a year after obtaining a bachelor's and/or master's degree and gaining supervised practice experience (four to five years of combined academic study and practice, or 900 hours of internship). Pay rises with experience to over $50,000. The job outlook is about average.

Emergency Medical Technicians

Emergency medical technicians (EMTs) ride ambulances to provide on-the-spot medical aid. Numbering 172,000 in 2000, they earn a median pay of $22,460 a year. Training comes in the form of special programs run by police and fire departments and hospitals and as special courses in medical schools, colleges, and universities. Every state requires certification. The job outlook is above average.

Health Service Managers

Subject to boards of directors and other governing groups, *medical* and *health service managers* manage clinics, hospitals, nursing homes, and other providers of medical care. They oversee budgets, rates, personnel, and planning; raise funds; and handle public relations. There are about 250,000 such managers, many of whom work long hours for pay that averages about $56,000 a year; the top 10 percent earn over $100,000. The education for the job can mean a bachelor's, master's, or doctorate in hospital or health administration or public health. One can also enter the field with a degree in personnel administration, public administration, or business. Competition for jobs is strong, and the higher degrees are essential for the best-paid positions. The strongest demand will be in managed-care operations, health maintenance organizations (HMOs), and nursing homes. Employment is expected to grow faster than average through at least 2010.

Licensed Practical Nurses

Licensed practical nurses (LPNs) provide hospital bedside care, assist physicians and registered nurses, administer medications, instruct patients, make appointments, and take medical histories. They number over 700,000, earn median annual salaries of about $30,000, and are graduates of one-year programs offered at technical, trade, and vocational schools; at community colleges; and in the military. Most schools require a high school diploma for admission. Employment is expected to rise about as fast as average through the year 2010.

Medical Assistants

Medical (or medical office) *assistants* serve as receptionists and as recorders of patient data, perform simple laboratory tests, prepare patients and instruments, and instruct patients. Most of the 329,000 in this country earn $23,000 a year. Most graduate from one- and two-year medical assistant programs offered by community colleges and vocational schools. Job growth is expected to be among the fastest growing through 2010.

Medical Record and Health Information Technicians

Medical record and *health information technicians* assemble and maintain patient records in doctors' offices, clinics, and hospitals. Numbering about 136,000, they transcribe, analyze, code, and file medical data; maintain registries; compile statistics; and abstract records. Their work is essential in dealing with medical insurance companies. In small institutions, they run the system. They need a two-year associate degree and average about $23,000 a year. Employment should grow much faster than average as the health field and its associated paperwork continue to expand.

Nuclear Medicine Technologists

Nuclear medicine technologists carry out diagnosis and treatment of disease using radioactive chemicals. They may also do research, implement safety procedures, and operate diagnostic imaging equipment (also a task of radiological technologists). In 2000, nuclear medicine technologists held about 18,000 jobs, mostly in hospitals. Training programs last from one to four years and culminate in a certificate or an associate or bachelor's degree. Pay averages about $44,000. Employment will grow faster than the average for all occupations through the year 2010.

Nursing, Psychiatric, and Home Health Aides

The nation's 2,100,000 *nursing, psychiatric,* and *home health aides* help care for the ill, the disabled, and the infirm. They work in hospitals, where they may also be known as orderlies, nursing assistants, or hospital attendants, and in nursing homes, where they may be called geriatric aides. Home health aides assist the elderly and disabled to live in their own homes instead of in nursing homes or other health-care facilities. They do housekeeping, personal care, and child care, provide emotional support, and even run errands. They work with social workers, nurses, and physical therapists. They often do not need even a high school diploma, although many employers do require training and certification. In 2000, pay averaged about $17,500 per year. The field will have an ample supply of openings through the year 2010. Jobs for home health aides will expand most rapidly.

Occupational Health and Safety Specialists and Technicians

The 35,000 *occupational health* and *safety specialists and technicians* inspect workplaces and equipment, promote workplace safety, and enforce occupational health and safety laws and regulations. Their duties vary widely, according to whether they work for industry or federal, state, or local government. Required training includes both a bachelor's degree and experience. Median pay is about $43,000. Employment is expected to increase about as fast as average through 2010.

Occupational Therapists

Occupational therapists work as part of a medical team to help patients develop independence, develop or regain skills, prepare to return to work, and adjust to disabilities. They need at least a bachelor's degree, must pass a national certification exam, number 78,000, and average about $50,000 a year. The job outlook through 2010 is very good.

Occupational Therapy Assistants/Aides

Occupational therapy assistants and *aides* work under the direction of occupational therapists. They provide rehabilitation services for patients with physical, mental, and developmental problems. Assistants work directly with patients; aides typically prepare materials, make appointments, and fill out insurance forms. There are about 17,000 assistants, who need at least an associate's degree, and have average earnings of about $34,000. Aides number 8,500, learn most of their skills on the job, and earn only $21,000.

Ophthalmic Laboratory Technicians/Optical Mechanics

Ophthalmic laboratory technicians, also know as *optical mechanics*, make prescription eyeglasses, following the prescription of an ophthalmologist, dispensing optician, or optometrist. The 32,000 in this occupation learned their skills on the job; through formal, three- to four-year apprenticeship programs; or through six-month to two-year programs at community colleges, vocational and technical institutes, or trade schools. Their median pay is approximately $20,000 per year. Job growth through the year 2010 is expected to be slow because automated equipment is doing an ever-larger part of the work.

Dispensing Opticians

Dispensing opticians accept eyeglass prescriptions, measure patients to fit eyeglasses, instruct ophthalmic lab technicians, and adjust the finished product. Numbering about 68,000, they learn their skills on the job, in two-year programs, and in a few shorter programs. Median earnings are $24,430 a year, with the best prospects for those who work in the offices of medical doctors (ophthalmologists). The job outlook for dispensing opticians is about average.

Optometrists

Optometrists diagnose eye problems and prescribe lenses and treatment, supply glasses, and fit and adjust glasses. The 31,000 practicing optometrists in this country each hold a four-year doctor of optometry degree from a college of optometry, on top of two or three years of preoptometric study at a college, university, or community college. (Many students enter colleges of optometry with a bachelor's degree in hand.) Salaried optometrists earned a median pay of $82,860 in 2000; those in private practice averaged $115,000 to $120,000 a year. The job outlook is favorable, with employment expected to grow about as fast as average through the year 2010.

Pharmacists

Pharmacists dispense drugs prescribed by physicians and dentists, maintain patient drug records, and advise customers on nonprescription medications. Of the 217,000 pharmacists working in 2000, most worked in community pharmacies (drugstores). To get their state license to practice pharmacy, pharmacists must study for at least five years beyond high school to gain a bachelor of science (B.S.) in pharmacy, serve an internship, and pass a state exam. A doctor of pharmacy degree requires at least one more year. Some pharmacy schools admit students directly from high school; most require one or two years of college first. In 2000, the median income of full-time salaried pharmacists was $71,000; those who worked for hospitals made a little less. Employment in this field is expected to grow faster than average through 2010.

Pharmacy Technicians

In 2000, 190,000 *pharmacy technicians* helped pharmacists prepare and dispense prescriptions to patients. The preferred training consists of two-year programs run by the military, hospitals, and two-year colleges. Pay is about $20,000 per year. The job outlook is better than average.

Physical Therapists

Physical therapists work with physicians and treat patients to restore bodily function, relieve pain, or prevent permanent disability after a disabling injury or disease. They number 132,000 and have bachelor's degrees; in 2002, all accredited programs also offered master's degrees. Most physical therapists work in hospitals. Median income in 2000 was almost $55,000. The job outlook is excellent.

Physical Therapy Assistants/Aides

Physical therapy assistants and *aides* need less education—a two-year degree for the former and a high school diploma for the latter. Some states require licensing. Numbering 80,000 in 2000, they work with therapists to instruct and assist patients. Median pay for assistants was about $34,000 in 2000; top pay exceeded $45,000. Aides averaged just under $20,000. Employment is expected to increase by 45 percent by 2010.

Physicians/Surgeons

Physicians diagnose and treat human illness and advise patients on its prevention. Some also do medical research. The 598,000 active U.S. physicians all have M.D. (doctor of medicine) or D.O. (doctor of osteopathy) degrees. M.D.s, who have graduated from medical schools, have spent at least four years of study to earn a bachelor's and another four to earn the M.D. Most have also spent three to eight years in a residency program, where they learned the additional skills necessary for a specialty in cardiology, surgery, pathology, neurology, internal medicine, ophthalmology, proctology, dermatology, obstetrics, and so on.

Osteopaths, who emphasize the muscles, bones, ligaments, and nerves of the human body and treat illness with manual manipulation as well as surgery, drugs, and other accepted medical tools, have completed three or four years at an osteopathic college. Osteopathic colleges require at least three years of college for admission, but most of their students have a full bachelor's degree. After graduation, most osteopaths spend a year as an intern and two to six years in a residency.

A new medical graduate, still in his or her residency program, can expect to earn $40,000 to $50,000 a year. After the residency, income shoots skyward, with the average physician making $160,000 in 1998; surgeons averaged $240,000. The job outlook through 2010 is very favorable, for the population is growing (albeit slowly), and there is a swelling proportion of elderly people, who require more medical attention.

Physician Assistants

Physician assistants take medical histories, perform medical exams, order lab tests, make tentative diagnoses, and prescribe treatments, while working under the supervision of physicians. The 58,000 in this occupation in 2000 were graduates of programs, often two years in length, in colleges, universities, medical schools, and community colleges; all states also require passing the Physician Assistants National Certifying Examination. The requirements for admission to these programs varied from a high school diploma to a bachelor's degree. In 2000, physician assistants averaged about $62,000 a year. Employment is expected to increase 53 percent by 2010.

Podiatrists

Podiatrists specialize in problems of the feet. They diagnose the problems and treat them with surgery, drugs, and corrective devices. The 18,000 active podiatrists are graduates of four-year colleges of podiatric medicine, which they entered after at least three years of college. They may also have served a one-year residency. All states require licensing. Median pay for salaried podiatrists was $107,560 in 2000; those in private practice made 10 to 12 percent less. The job outlook is about average through 2010.

Radiological Technologists/Technicians

The nation's 167,000 *radiological technologists* and *technicians* use X-rays and other imaging techniques to picture and diagnose problems within the human body. They may also use radiation to treat cancers and other illnesses. Subspecialties include radiographers (who use, for example, diagnostic X-rays, computerized tomography, and magnetic resonance imaging), radiation therapy technologists (who treat cancer with radiation), and sonographers or ultrasound technologists (who use sonar-like high-frequency sound waves to scan the body's interior). Training programs range in length from one to four years and result in a certificate, an associate degree, or a bachelor's degree; the associate degree is the most common. The median salary is $36,000. Employment should grow faster than the average for all occupations through the year 2010.

Recreational Therapists

Recreational therapists, sometimes called *therapeutic recreation specialists*, number 29,000. Most work in nursing homes and psychiatric and rehabilitation hospitals, where they use leisure activities as treatment for the mentally, physically, and emotionally disabled. They thus resemble occupational therapists. Formal training is required for entry into this field, and there are 160 college and university programs available, most offering bachelor's degrees. Associate degrees (enough for many nursing home jobs), master's, and doctoral degrees are also available. Pay varies, with nursing home positions averaging only $23,000 a year; overall, recreational therapists earn a median pay of $28,650 a year. Employment is expected to expand more slowly than the average for all occupations through the year 2010.

Registered Nurses

Registered nurses are famous for the quality they contribute to hospital care. They monitor patient progress, administer medications, teach health care, and maintain an atmosphere conducive to recovery. Registered nurses may also work in private homes, schools, community and industrial clinics, and physicians' offices. They may also teach on campus. They numbered 2.2

million in 2000. Registered nurses have graduated from a two-year associate degree (A.D.N.) program, a two- to three-year "diploma" program, or a four- to five-year bachelor's degree (B.S.N.) program and have passed a national license exam. A bachelor's degree is generally essential for supervisory positions. Master's and doctorate programs are also available. Some post-bachelor's programs equip registered nurses to become nurse practitioners, who have added diagnostic and assessment responsibilities in pediatrics, geriatrics, mental health, midwifery, and medical-surgical nursing. The pay averages about $45,000 a year, with supervisory nurses making over $60,000. The job prospects are very good, with employment expected to increase by 26 percent by 2010.

Respiratory Therapists

The nation's 110,000 *respiratory therapists* treat patients with heart and breathing problems. Most work in hospitals, but the number of positions in clinics and nursing homes is expanding. Respiratory therapists provide temporary relief to asthma and emphysema victims and emergency care to victims of heart failure, stroke, drowning, shock, poisoning, and head injury. Most therapists gain their training in two-year associate programs; bachelor's degrees are also available. Technicians usually have a certificate from a one-year program. The median income for therapists in 2000 was $37,680. The job outlook is well above average.

Social Workers

The nation's 468,000 *social workers* help people deal with mental, emotional, marital, and economic troubles. They work in welfare agencies, mental health clinics, alcohol and drug abuse clinics, and elsewhere. Many have only a bachelor's degree in the field. Higher-level positions require a master's. Pay varies; child, family, and school social workers employed by elementary and secondary schools had median earnings of $41,700 in 2000; those employed in residential care had a median pay of only $26,780. Median pay for medical and public health social workers employed by hospitals was $40,020; those employed in individual and family services earned $29,730. The job outlook is better than average, although it is more than usually subject to fluctuations in public policy. Employment prospects are best in urban areas.

Speech-Language Pathologists and Audiologists

Speech-language pathologists and *audiologists* strive to diagnose and remedy or compensate for defects in speech and hearing. They number 101,000, and their standard credential is a master's degree. Median income in 2000 was $46,640. Employment should increase much faster than average until the year 2010.

Surgical Technologists

In 2000, 71,000 men and women worked as *surgical technologists*, preparing operating rooms and patients for surgery, passing equipment to surgeons, handling specimens, and working sterilizers, lights, suction machines, and diagnostic equipment. Most community college, hospital, and vocational and technical school training programs last nine to twenty-four months. Pay averages about $29,000 annually. The job outlook is better than average.

Veterinarians

Veterinarians are specialists in the prevention, diagnosis, and treatment of animal diseases and injuries. Numbering 59,000 in 2000, they have four-year degrees from colleges of veterinary medicine, as well as state licenses. Most veterinary students already have a bachelor's degree; all veterinary schools require at least two years of college for admission. Veterinarians employed by the federal government averaged $67,482 per year in 2001. Overall, the median pay for veterinarians in 2000 was $61,000. Employment is expected to grow faster than average through the year 2010.

SOCIAL SCIENCES

Economists and Market and Survey Researchers

The nation's 134,000 *economists* and *market* and *survey researchers* study and interpret the interactions of labor, raw materials, finance, and finished goods to describe and predict the behavior of the economy as a whole. Many specialize in labor, transportation, marketing, energy, agriculture, or other fields and advise government, business, unions, and financial institutions. Market research analysts focus on marketing, analyzing statistics to predict sales and make recommendations to their employers. Survey researchers design and conduct surveys, working with economists, market research analysts, politicians, and others. A third of all economists work in colleges and universities. The best jobs go to economists with doctorates, but jobs exist for those with bachelor's and master's degrees as well.

In 2000, the median pay for economists was $64,830; for market research analysts, $51,190; for survey researchers, $26,200. In the federal government, economists with bachelor's degrees start at about $21,900 per year, those with master's degrees at about $33,300 per year, and those with doctoral degrees at about $40,200 per year. Economists working in the federal government average over $74,900. Employment of economists and market and survey researchers should grow faster than the average for all occupations through the year 2010.

Psychologists

The nation's 182,000 *psychologists* are students of human behavior. Clinical psychologists serve the needs of the mentally and emotionally disturbed. Other specialties include developmental, experimental, personality, comparative, social, physiological, educational, counseling, school, industrial, engineering, and community psychology. Psychologists who choose a life of research and teaching in colleges and universities need a doctorate; so do clinical psychologists in many states. A master's degree may be enough for community college teaching, psychological testing, and other jobs.

In 2000, salaried psychologists earned a median pay of $48,596; those working for hospitals made the most, with a median of $52,460 per year. In the federal government, psychologists with bachelor's degrees start at about $21,900 per year, those with master's degrees at about $33,300 per year, and those with doctoral degrees at about $40,200 per year. Psychologists in the federal government averaged $72,830 in 2001. Employment of psychologists should grow as fast as the average for all occupations through the year 2010.

Social Scientists

Social scientists study human society in all its aspects—past and present—to help us understand how people make decisions, wield power, and respond to change and to the need for change. They include 15,000 anthropologists, archaeologists, geographers, historians, political scientists, and sociologists who work for government agencies, research organizations, consulting firms, businesses, health facilities, and so on. Still more work as faculty members for colleges and universities.

Social scientists as a whole averaged about $48,000 per year in 2000. Political scientists did best, with a median pay of $81,000. In the federal government, starting pay for bachelor's graduates was about $22,000; for master's graduates, $33,000; and for doctorates, $40,000. Employment of social scientists should expand about as fast as average through the year 2010. Competition will be strong, especially in academia, and the prospects are best for those with advanced degrees.

Urban and Regional Planners

Urban and *regional planners* aid city, county, and state governments in selecting, siting, and building new medical, educational, and other facilities to meet the needs of the locality. They number 30,000, and most entry-level jobs require a master's degree or its equivalent in experience. The pay averages over $46,500 a year. Employment should increase about as fast as the average for all occupations through the year 2010.

ORGANIZATIONS FOR HELPING AND SOCIAL SCIENTISTS

There are a great many organizations for those who work in the helping and social sciences. Most provide journals, career information, and other services to members. Some, such as the American Medical Association and American Sociological Association, run periodic professional meetings where researchers give presentations and employers can meet potential employees.

Because the specifics vary tremendously, interested readers should consult the websites listed for the following organizations.

Societies and Sources of Further Information for Careers in Helping and Social Sciences

Alliance of Cardiovascular Professionals
4456 Corporation Lane, Suite 165
Virginia Beach, VA 23462
www.acp-online.org

American Academy of Physicians Assistants
950 N. Washington Street
Alexandria, VA 22314-1552
www.aapa.org

American Anthropological Association
4350 N. Fairfax Drive, Suite 640
Arlington, VA 22203-1620
www.aaanet.org

American Association for Marriage and Family Therapy
112 South Alfred Street
Alexandria, VA 22314-3061
www.aamft.org/index_nm.asp

American Association for Respiratory Care
11030 Ables Lane
Dallas, TX 75229-4593
www.aarc.org

American Association of Colleges of Pharmacy
1426 Prince Street
Alexandria, VA 22314
www.aacp.org

American Association of Medical Assistants
20 N. Wacker Drive, Suite 1575
Chicago, IL 60606
www.aama-ntl.org

American Chiropractic Association
1701 Clarendon Boulevard
Arlington, VA 22209
www.amerchiro.org

American College of Health Care Administrators
1800 Diagonal Road, Suite 355
Alexandria, VA 22314
www.achca.org

American Counseling Association
5999 Stevenson Avenue
Alexandria, VA 22304
www.counseling.org

American Dental Assistants Association
203 N. LaSalle Street, Suite 1320
Chicago, IL 60601
www.dentalassistant.org

American Dental Association
211 E. Chicago Avenue
Chicago, IL 60611
www.ada.org

American Dietetic Association
216 W. Jackson Boulevard, Suite 800
Chicago, IL 60606-6995
www.eatright.org

American Health Care Association
1201 L Street, NW
Washington, DC 20005
www.ahca.org

American Health Information Management Association
233 N. Michigan Avenue, Suite 2150
Chicago, IL 60601-5800
www.ahima.org

American Industrial Hygiene Association
2700 Prosperity Avenue, Suite 250
Fairfax, VA 22031
www.aiha.org

American Medical Association
515 N. State Street
Chicago, IL 60610
www.ama-assn.org

American Mental Health Counselors Association
801 N. Fairfax Street, Suite 304
Alexandria, VA 22314
www.amhca.org

American Nurses Association
600 Maryland Avenue, SW
Washington, DC 20024-2571
www.nursingworld.org

American Occupational Therapy Association
4720 Montgomery Lane
P.O. Box 31220
Bethesda, MD 20824-1220
www.aota.org

American Optometric Association
243 N. Lindbergh Boulevard
St. Louis, MO 63141-7881
www.aoanet.org

American Osteopathic Association
142 East Ontario Street
Chicago, IL 60611
www.aoa-net.org

American Physical Therapy Association
1111 N. Fairfax Street
Alexandria, VA 22314-1488
www.apta.org

American Planning Association
1776 Massachusetts Avenue, NW
Washington, DC 20036-1904
www.planning.org

American Podiatric Medical Association
9312 Old Georgetown Road
Bethesda, MD 20814-1621
www.apma.org

American Psychiatric Association
1000 Wilson Boulevard, Suite 1825
Arlington, VA 22209-3901
www.psych.org

American Psychological Association
750 First Street, NE
Washington, DC 20002-4242
www.apa.org

American Rehabilitation Counseling Association
5999 Stevenson Avenue
Alexandria, VA 22304-3300
www.nchrtm.okstate.edu/arca

American Society for Clinical Laboratory Science
7910 Woodmont Avenue, Suite 530
Bethesda, MD 20814
www.ascp.org

American Society of Electroneurodiagnostic Technologists, Inc.
426 W. 42nd Street
Kansas City, MO 64111
www.aset.org

American Society of Radiologic Technologists
15000 Central Avenue, SE
Albuquerque, NM 87123-3917
www.asrt.org/asrt.htm

American Sociological Association
1307 New York Avenue, NW, Suite 700
Washington, DC 20005-4712
www.asanet.org

American Speech-Language-Hearing Association
10801 Rockville Pike
Rockville, MD 20852
www.professional.asha.org

American Veterinary Medical Association
1931 N. Meacham Road, Suite 100
Schaumburg, IL 60173-4360
www.avma.org

Association of American Geographers
1710 16th Street, NW
Washington, DC 20009-3198
www.aag.org

Association of Surgical Technologists
7108-C S. Alton Way
Englewood, CO 80112
www.ast.org

Marketing Research Association
1344 Silas Deane Highway, Suite 306
Rocky Hill, CT 06067-0230
www.mra-net.org

National Association for Business Economists
1233 20th Street, NW, Suite 505
Washington, DC 20036
www.nabe.com

National Association for Home Care and Hospice
228 7th Street, SE
Washington, DC 20003
www.nahc.org

National Association of Dental Laboratories
1530 Metropolitan Boulevard
Tallahassee, FL 32308
www.nadl.org

National Association of Emergency Medical Technicians
408 Monroe Street
Clinton, MS 39056
www.naemt.org

National Association of Social Workers
750 First Street, NE, Suite 700
Washington, DC 20002-4241
www.naswdc.org

National League for Nursing
61 Broadway
New York, NY 10006
www.nln.org

National Rehabilitation Counseling Association
8807 Sudley Road, Suite 102
Manassas, VA 22110-4719
nrca-net.org

National Therapeutic Recreation Society
22377 Belmont Ridge Road
Ashburn, VA 20148-4501
www.nrpa.org/branches/ntrs.htm

Opticians Association of America
7023 Little River Turnpike, Suite 207
Annandale, VA 22003
www.opticians.org

Society for American Archeology
900 2nd Street, NE, Suite 12
Washington, DC 20002-3557
www.saa.org

Society of Diagnostic Medical Sonographers
12770 Coit Road, Suite 708
Dallas, TX 75251
www.sdms.org

Society of Nuclear Medicine—Technologist Section
1850 Samuel Morse Drive
Reston, VA 22090
www.snm.org

CHAPTER 5

CAREERS IN LIFE SCIENCES

Many careers in the helping sciences deal in applications of the life sciences to human health. The helping sciences are thus applied versions of the life sciences, though they are not the only ones. The life sciences, the many branches of biology, can also be applied to agriculture and to industrial production. Every branch has both a results-oriented, applied side and a "pure," curiosity-satisfying basic research side.

The distinction between pure and applied work has far more to do with the setting and goal of one's work than with its content. In pure research, microbiologists work to understand the lives of microorganisms. They may or may not teach, collect soil samples in the wilderness, or do other things. Their lab may be associated with a university, a drug company, or a government agency. Applications-oriented microbiologists may work in these same places or for a hospital or public health agency or even—ever since the anthrax scare of 2001—for law enforcement agencies. They study microorganisms to find new antibiotics; to improve the production of beer, wine, or bread; to find causes of and treatments for diseases; or to develop ways of detecting microorganisms in the food supply, the environment, and the body. They may also strive to identify suspicious powders or other substances. Both pure and applied microbiologists work with the same organisms and the same techniques.

About 40 percent of all life scientists work for federal, state, or local government agencies. The rest are found on college and university campuses and in private industry. Wherever they work, they are involved in research and development, data collection, food and drug testing, and more. Some teach classes or disseminate information through agricultural extension services. Some manage research programs, university departments, regulatory agencies, testing labs, zoos, museums, and botanical gardens. Some are inspectors of food and drugs, consultants to business and government, technical writers, and technical sales and service representatives. Some—particularly in the new and growing biotechnology industry—are entrepreneurs. All must know research techniques and be able to use laboratory equipment and procedures.

It may be simplest to approach the life science careers in terms of the many fields of biology, the specialties a life scientist can move into. We cannot cover every biological specialty here, but we can discuss a few.

Later in this chapter, we will look at the careers available on campus, in industry and business, and in government. We will identify those areas where the pace of discovery is swift, the excitement of the workers is greatest, and the promise of the work for society is highest. Finally, we will list a few of the many organizations to which life scientists may belong and from which career information is available.

The life sciences are split into three broad fields that overlap to some extent. These fields are the agricultural and food sciences, conservation science and forestry, and the biological and medical sciences.

AGRICULTURAL AND FOOD SCIENCES

Agricultural and food scientists, numbering 17,000 in 2000 (several thousand more are found on campus), apply their knowledge of biology and other sciences to the production of food, fiber, and various other materials grown on farms. *Agronomists* and *crop scientists* work to improve the yield and quality of crops, such as corn, soybeans, and cotton, by developing new ways to grow them or to control pests such as weeds and insects; they also develop new varieties of crop plants. Today this may involve the controversial techniques of genetic engineering. *Horticulturalists* do the same for orchard and garden plants, which are usually grown on a smaller scale, and add an emphasis on plants used in landscaping. *Soil scientists* study the composition, structure, and distribution of soil and advise farmers on how to control erosion and other soil problems. *Animal scientists* focus on the breeding, growth, and care of farm animals; *veterinarians* are animal scientists whose purview includes pets, farm animals, and animals kept in zoos (see Chapter 4). *Food scientists* or *technologists* work to improve methods of processing, preserving, packaging, distributing, storing, and preparing foods; they work in basic research, applied research, and quality control.

Doctoral-level agricultural scientists can expect good employment opportunities through the year 2010, but employment opportunities are expected to expand more slowly than the average for all occupations. Bachelor's graduates will find more competition for jobs, as well as lower pay. Median pay in 2000 was $52,160. In 2001, new bachelor's graduates in animal science received average offers of $28,000 a year. In the federal government, animal scientists averaged $76,581 in salary in 2001; agronomists averaged $62,311; soil scientists averaged $58,878; horticulturalists averaged $59,472; and entomologists averaged $70,133.

Job opportunities in agricultural science may be greatest in private industry, for despite public resistance to "genetically modified" crops, the rapid development of biotechnology (genetic engineering) has already brought pest- and herbicide-resistant soybeans, corn, and other crops to both farm and supermarket, and nutritionally enhanced crops are in the offing. In the future, we can expect demand to rise rapidly as soil fertility and water supply for irrigation decline and food production fails to keep up with world population growth.

CONSERVATION SCIENCE AND FORESTRY

For now, the job prospects for *foresters* and *conservation scientists* look less than optimistic; job growth is expected to be slower than the average for all occupations through 2010. Growth will be strongest in state and local government thanks to efforts to protect the environment. Growth will probably be less at the federal level, despite growing need in the areas of soil and water conservation.

Foresters plan and supervise the planting, growing, protection, and harvesting of trees, which we use for fuel, lumber, paper, and even chemical feedstocks. They plant, map, inventory, and fight fire, pests, and disease. They may also deal in wildlife protection, watershed management, and the development and supervision of camps, parks, and grazing lands. Most are employed by private industry. Because of intense job competition among foresters with no more than a bachelor's degree, higher degrees are advisable and are in fact essential for managerial, teaching, and research positions.

Soil conservationists help farmers and other land managers use their land as productively as possible without damaging it. They recommend the best uses of land and cultivation methods that will prevent erosion and maintain or improve fertility, monitor water supplies, and develop water conservation measures. Most have a bachelor's degree in agronomy, general agriculture, or crop or soil science or in a related field, such as wildlife biology, forestry, or range management.

Range managers work to improve and protect rangelands or to maximize their use without damage. Rangelands are found mostly in the western United States, where they serve for animal grazing, wildlife habitats, water catchment areas, and recreation. Like foresters, range managers with ambitions for managerial, teaching, or research positions need a graduate degree.

In 2000, there were about 29,000 foresters and conservation scientists, about 40 percent of whom worked for the federal government. Another 25 percent worked for state governments, and 10 percent worked for cities, towns, and counties. The rest worked for private industry or as self-employed consultants.

In 2000, the median pay for conservation scientists was $47,140; for foresters, $43,640. In 2001, the federal government hired bachelor's graduates at $23,776 or $30,035 a year (depending on their grades). Master's graduates started at $30,357 or $42,783. Doctorates began at $52,162 unless they were in research, where the pay began at $61,451. The average nonsupervisory federal forester made $55,006 in 2001; the average soil conservationist made $53,591. Offers to new graduates with a bachelor's degree in conservation or renewable natural resources averaged $28,571.

The job outlook for *biological* and *medical scientists* is very good, although there will be intense competition for research jobs. The number of available positions should grow faster than the average for all occupations through the year 2010. Among the sources of new jobs will be the genetic engineering and biotechnology industries, which are already bringing products—including modified crops; gene replacement therapies; drugs produced in genetically engineered organisms; tests for genes associated with hereditary diseases, including cancer; artificial organs; and more—to market. Protecting the environment and restoring portions of the environment damaged in the past will also call for a great many workers. The environmental industry accounted for about 3 million jobs in 2000, although not all of them were for scientists. There is also a large need for biological researchers and technicians in the study of the human (and other) genome, the search for a cure or treatment for acquired immune deficiency syndrome (AIDS), and other areas.

The biological sciences are relatively recession-proof, for a great many jobs are in teaching, long-term research, and agriculture. However, because about 40 percent of biological scientists are employed by federal, state, and local government agencies, they are vulnerable to budget cutbacks. Fortunately, a degree in the life sciences is excellent preparation for a shift into the health fields.

In 2000, there were 138,000 biological and medical scientists, with thousands more teaching at colleges and universities. Biological scientists enjoyed median salaries of $49,239. Medical scientists averaged $57,196. New graduates with a bachelor's degree in biological science could start at $29,235 per year; new master's graduates could start at $35,667; and new doctorates could start at $42,744. In 2001, biologists employed by the federal government averaged $61,236. Microbiologists earned $67,835, ecologists $61,936, physiologists $78,366, and geneticists $72,510. Top-ranked researchers are in another ballpark entirely, for their pay can exceed $250,000 per year.

The doctorate is essential for most positions in college teaching, independent research, and management. Medical scientists may need a medical degree in addition. The master's degree will do for some jobs in applied research, such as research assistant, field technician, or laboratory technician. A bachelor's degree qualifies one for some technician positions, for jobs in sales and service, and for support positions such as technical writer. High school biology teachers often have a bachelor's degree in biology, with added education courses.

Most working biological scientists are less concerned with food, fiber, and raw material production than are agricultural scientists. They define their subject areas less in terms of human needs than in terms of life itself and the categories into which living things fall and the levels of biological function. Biological scientists thus include zoologists, botanists, anatomists, physiologists, and geneticists.

Zoologists are engaged in the scientific study of animals. Their field encompasses taxonomy, or systematics—the identification, description, and classification of animals; mammalogy, the study of mammals; ichthyology, the study of fishes; herpetology, the study of reptiles; entomology, the study of insects; protozoology, the study of protozoa; and so on. A zoologist who emphasizes the economic impact of insects is an economic entomologist. One who studies disease-causing protozoa is a medical protozoologist. One who focuses on the interrelationships of animals with one another and with their environment is an ecologist. If one studies hormones, one is an endocrinologist; behavior, an ethologist; parasites, a parasitologist; evolution, an evolutionary biologist. As an anatomist, one studies the structure of animals. As a physiologist, one focuses on growth, metabolism, reproduction, respiration, and movement. A geneticist studies genes and heredity. Biochemists and molecular biologists study the cell at the level of the molecules that make up the cell. Today, many molecular biologists are also geneticists, for some of those molecules are those of the genes, and genome studies and genetic engineering are a major center of attention.

Where the zoologist is concerned with animals in all their aspects, the *botanist* is concerned with plants. A botanist can specialize in single kinds of plants or in single aspects of their biology. Some botanists focus on ferns, mosses, or trees; on taxonomy, evolution, or genetics; on growth regulation, metabolism, photosynthesis, ecology, reproduction, or biochemistry.

Virologists study viruses—how they infect cells, how they cause disease, and how their victims can be cured or treated.

Microbiologists concentrate on microorganisms—on bacteria, yeasts, fungi, protozoa, and one-celled algae. The microbiologist, too, can be a taxonomist, geneticist, physiologist, ecologist, or evolutionary biologist. Often, he or she is interested in applications, for bacteria, yeasts, and fungi are used to produce foods such as wine, beer, bread, cheese, soy sauce, and tofu; antibiotics; and industrial chemicals. Equipped with new genes (recombinant DNA), microorganisms now produce hormones and other drugs for medical use. Because many microorganisms cause disease, some microbiologists are concerned with diagnosis, treatment, and prevention; they are medical microbiologists.

Physiologists are concerned with how organisms work, how they respond to changes in their external and internal environments, in both health and disease. Physiologists thus seek an understanding of the basic physical and chemical mechanisms of all of life. They not only want to know what happens inside a plant, animal, or cell, but also want to know how and why it happens. There are general, mammalian, comparative, plant, reproductive, and environmental physiologists, among others.

Pharmacologists are concerned with how drugs work. They are thus a kind of physiologist, but with a bent toward health applications. Also a biochemist, the pharmacologist works with "pure" biochemists who use the pharmacologist's understanding of drug action to probe the dynamics of cellular chemistry.

The *biochemist* studies the effects of foods, hormones, drugs, and toxins on plants, animals, and single cells. His or her aim is to know what chemical compounds make up living things and how they interact in metabolism, growth, reproduction, and heredity. The biochemist may be a basic researcher or an applied researcher working in medicine, agriculture, or industry. Many of today's biochemists work for biotechnology firms and strive to synthesize and produce on a large scale such biological chemicals as enzymes and antibiotics.

Ecologists are concerned with the interrelationships between organisms and their environments. Interdisciplinary by nature, ecology encompasses many areas of biology, chemistry, geology, meteorology, and climatology. It contributes to our ability to understand and forestall disastrous effects of human activities, volcanic eruptions, and climate changes on our air, water, and food supplies. It also challenges our accustomed view of ourselves as independent of the world around us, and it has amply earned its sobriquet as "the subversive science."

Ecology is the parent of the *environmental sciences* that deal with the problems that arise because of humanity's interactions with the world on which it lives. Here we find a number of occupations whose members try to prevent or cope with crises. There are, for instance, some 52,000 *environmental engineers*, and the American Academy of Environmental Engineers reports that pay starts at $36,000 to $42,000 for bachelor's graduates, $40,000 to $45,000 for master's graduates, and $42,000 to $50,000 for doctorates. As in many environmental careers, job satisfaction is high, and job prospects are excellent for the foreseeable future. *Environmental epidemiologists* study the connection between environmental factors and disease. Since demand for these specialists exceeds supply, the job prospects are excellent.

Other environmental occupations include natural resource managers, environmental trainers, emergency responders, and even environmental lawyers. A less formal specialty is environmental management. In the past, this has been a synonym for sanitation engineering (sewage and garbage processing), but at some schools it refers to the interface between business and environmental concerns.

Ethologists study animal behavior. Unlike psychology, ethology is more observational than experimental. It also seeks to understand the adaptive, evolutionary bases for human and animal actions.

Immunologists study how the body defends itself against invasion by foreign substances, such as those carried on the surfaces of disease organisms and the cells of transplanted organs. Immunology's greatest gift to medicine to date is vaccines, but it may have greater ones in store. Immunologists study the production of antibodies—proteins that attach to foreign molecules—and the activities of immune system cells that attack and kill foreign cells. From their efforts have come ways to produce pure antibodies (with "hybridomas") and stimulate or suppress the immune system. Soon they may give us better treatments for cancer, more reliable organ transplants, and better relief from allergies. They may even find better ways to treat—or even cure—viral infections such as herpes and AIDS (acquired immune deficiency syndrome). Certainly they are trying.

Geneticists study heredity, and they have taught the world how to breed improved crop plants and animals. They were thus responsible for the "Green Revolution" that has helped to feed the burgeoning millions of the developing countries. Geneticists have also discovered the substance of the gene, DNA, and learned how to transplant genes from one organism to another. The study of DNA and its action is often better known as molecular biology. The gene transplant work has given rise to the field of genetic engineering, and genetic engineering companies are now manufacturing hormones, enzymes, and proteins for medical and industrial use. The future may yield new foods, improved varieties of plants and animals, crop plants that need less fertilizer, and cures for hereditary diseases.

A great many geneticists remain basic researchers who study how various characteristics pass from parent to offspring. They usually study short-generation organisms, such as viruses, bacteria, and fruit flies, although some study humans. *Human geneticists* have provided new explanations for such mental disorders as schizophrenia and depression. They are also concerned with the treatment and prediction of birth defects and heritable diseases such as Huntington's chorea. To aid this effort, the 1990s saw a massive effort to map the human genome, identifying all human genes and pinning down their locations on the chromosomes. Now researchers are mapping the genomes of other creatures for comparison purposes. This effort has already resulted in the ability to test for many disease genes and made clear the functions of many others; it has also raised a number of important ethical questions. Other geneticists work as *genetic counselors*, advising people with a family history of genetic defects of their chances of having normal children.

There are many other fields of biological science, but those described here are enough to show the great breadth of the area and to suggest that a career here can have an enormous amount of variety. Most biological scientists split their time among research, teaching, administration, and writing. Some split theirs between university and industry or government. Others work full-time for the government, for an educational institution, for a private research outfit, or for a zoo, botanical garden, or museum. There are biologists everywhere, and they do just about everything that relates to life.

SCIENCE TECHNICIANS

Research in the life sciences and in the earth, physical, space, and computer sciences, as well as in engineering and mathematics, is not a matter only for Ph.D. researchers. These men and women need the assistance of a horde of technicians who do much of the hands-on work of research. These technicians design, build, and operate equipment, run tests, and process information. Outside of research, they work in product development, production, sales, and customer service; they also search for various resources (such as water, oil, and minerals) and help make them available for use.

In 2000, there were about 198,000 agricultural, food science, biological, chemical, forest, conservation, forensic, environmental, geological, meteorological, museum, nuclear, petroleum, and other science technicians (519,000 engineering technicians are counted separately; see Chapter 9). According to the Bureau of Labor Statistics, about 37 percent worked in manufacturing, largely in the food-processing, chemical, and energy industries. Another 40 percent worked in academic settings and independent R&D laboratories. Government employed 29,000. Overall, employment should increase about as fast as the average for all occupations through the year 2010.

Science technicians are qualified for their jobs by two-year degrees in specific technologies and by Armed Forces training programs. Bachelor's graduates with a science background can also become technicians. In 2000, science technicians averaged about $35,000 per year, with hourly earnings ranging from $13 (for agricultural and food science technicians) to $28.44 (for nuclear technicians). Technicians in the life sciences earned less than those in the physical sciences. In 2001, federal pay began at $17,483 to $22,251, depending on education and experience.

HOT SPOTS

The 1990s were renowned as the decade of the computer. Computer technology exploded, new businesses proliferated, fortunes were made, and almost every life was affected. The first decade or two of the twenty-first century is already being hailed as the era of biotechnology. The environmental sciences are and will remain very active. The excitement of new discovery will come to the geneticists, biochemists, and molecular biologists who are mapping human, mouse, chimpanzee, corn, rice, and other genomes, developing techniques for manipulating the genes, and applying the new knowledge to questions of human health and agricultural productivity. These scientists will affect medicine, agriculture, and industry profoundly, and the inventions and processes they devise will make many of them wealthy. More excitement will come to the immunologists who develop vaccines and cancer treatments and to the developmental biologists who work with embryonic stem cells to develop therapies for Alzheimer's, Parkinson's, and other patients.

In its January/February 2001 issue, the magazine *Technology Review* listed "Ten Emerging Technologies That Will Change the World," including brain-machine interfaces and biometrics (identification by body features such as eye and face patterns). In the January/February 2003 issue, the magazine listed injectable tissue engineering, molecular imaging, and glycomics (sugar-related substances as drugs). Several of these technologies marry the life sciences to computers and electronics, but it is clear that the life sciences have a major role to play in shaping our lives over the next few decades.

Perhaps not surprisingly, many of the new technologies—genetic engineering, cloning, stem cells, and even personalized medications (based on genome studies)—are proving controversial. There is thus growing demand for ethicists (bioethicists), counselors (genetic counselors), philosophers, and even pastors with an understanding of the life sciences.

In most areas, the excitement will be less in the work than in the worker, for most biologists are drawn to their field by experiences with parents, early teachers, and mentors. They work more for the love of the work than for love of rewards such as money.

CAREERS ON CAMPUS

A great many doctoral-level life scientists work for educational institutions, where their pay is adequate, if not luxurious. In 2000, university instructors made an average of $34,700; assistant professors, $45,600; associate professors, $55,300; and full professors, $76,200.

There are more than 1,344,000 college and university faculty members, 30 percent of them part-time or "adjunct." The Bureau of Labor Statistics expects this number to grow by 23 percent, faster than the average for all occupations, between 2000 and 2010 as older faculty members retire, as the number of college-age young people continues to increase, and as more adults return to school. There will also be an increase in the number of foreign-born students.

It seems likely that the competition for academic jobs will remain strong and that a single job advertisement will still draw hundreds of applications. The fields with the best career prospects must therefore be those that offer attractive nonacademic employment opportunities. Several in the sciences fill the bill: engineering, health science, computer science, physical sciences, and mathematics. Many life scientists, with and without doctoral degrees, will continue to find employment as high school biology teachers.

Except in two-year schools, college and university life scientists are generally expected to be both teacher and researcher. However, their duties are hardly restricted to lecturing, supervising student laboratories, and doing their own research. They must also keep up with advances in their field by reading and attending scientific meetings, writing grant proposals to gain funding for their research, and writing up the results of their research as papers and books. In addition, they must serve on faculty committees.

College and university life scientists must have doctorates if they expect to advance beyond the level of instructor. Once they have obtained this degree, they may begin their working careers as "postdocs." They join the research team of a senior researcher in their field to concentrate on research and gain skills free from the demands of teaching and committee work.

The National Research Council has called the postdoc "an important period of transition between formal education and a career in research." And in *Enhancing the Postdoctoral Experience for Scientists and Engineers,* the Committee on Science, Engineering, and Public Policy of the National Academy of Sciences, National Academy of Engineering, and Institute of Medicine wrote: "The primary purpose of the postdoctoral experience is to broaden and deepen the research and other skills that are required for a significant contribution to society and satisfying, professional employment. Ideally, this is accomplished through the guidance of an adviser in whose laboratory or department the postdoc works; the administrative and infrastructural support of the host institution; the financial support of a funding organization; and the professional development support of a disciplinary society." At the same time, "the postdoctoral population has become indispensable to the science and engineering enterprise, performing a substantial portion of the nation's research in every setting."

Postdoctoral positions are found not only on campus but also in government and industrial laboratories. They do not include appointments in residency training programs in the health professions. By 2000, there were over 50,000 postdocs in all fields. A postdoc experience is still seen as essential for a research career, and it may last for several years. In some cases, it becomes a career in its own right, for many doctoral graduates find themselves forced to take second and third postdoctoral appointments when they fail to find positions as independent researchers or tenure-track faculty members or to obtain their own research grants. And their postdocs are not always in academic research labs. Some are with large corporate labs.

The life sciences account for the majority of postdocs, with about 60 percent of new doctorates taking such positions. Only about 17 percent give as their reason for taking a postdoc position the wish for additional training; almost 40 percent cite the lack of other employment in their field. Salaries average close to those of instructors ($30,000 in 1999) and are significantly less than those of new doctorates who find faculty positions. Relatively low pay is but one of the problems with postdoctoral employment; see the website of the National Postdoctoral Association (nationalpostdoc.org).

With or without a postdoc, a life scientist's first academic position may be that of instructor, perhaps while he or she is still a graduate student. Later come the positions of assistant professor, associate professor, and full professor, the last carrying the job security of "tenure," which protects against arbitrary dismissal and abolishes the worry over whether a contract will be renewed. On the way to full professorship, many life scientists move from school to school around the country. It often seems that whether one works in academia, industry, or government, one's present employer never recognizes one's true worth. Promotion comes faster with a change in job.

Nonfaculty positions on campus also exist for life scientists. University and college medical centers and clinics employ the full range of health personnel. Museums hire naturalists, taxonomists, collectors, and curators.

They focus on research, but they also teach courses to the general public (including students). *Curators* also administer their museums. *Museum exhibitors* conceive, plan, design, and set up the exhibits with which a museum speaks to the public. They are generalists well grounded in general biology, ecology, conservation, geology, geography, paleontology, anthropology, and principles of design. *Technical assistants* need only a bachelor's degree in biology.

Some universities are associated with their own or municipal zoos, botanical gardens, and arboretums. They employ veterinarians, plant and animal breeders, geneticists, ecologists, ethologists, and others who can help collect, preserve, and organize living and dead specimens from all over the world. Bachelor's and master's graduates may serve as gardeners, groundskeepers, horticulturists, caretakers, animal keepers, exhibit preparers, writers, editors, and librarians. The pay is comparable to that for faculty members.

Private research laboratories may be on or near campus, affiliated with or run by one or more universities, or totally independent. For example, the collection of labs at Research Triangle Park in North Carolina has a multiuniversity affiliation, whereas the Jackson Laboratory in Bar Harbor, Maine, famed for its work in mouse genetics and cancer research, is totally independent. Private research laboratories hire life scientists of all kinds as researchers, technicians, and administrators. They provide a pleasant, stable work environment, and they pay as well as most universities.

CAREERS IN INDUSTRY

Where life scientists on campus teach and do basic and applied research, those who work for private companies in industry do mainly applied research. They seek answers with immediate, practical uses. Their purpose is to support their employers' efforts to make a profit.

Industry performs a large amount of the nation's research and development work. Indeed, in 2000, industry funded two-thirds ($181 billion) of the total R&D bill, while the federal government covered only 26 percent; for basic research, industry covered 32 percent, the federal government 22 percent, and universities and colleges 43 percent. Life scientists find employment in the following industries:

- Aerospace companies
- Biological testing companies
- Collectors, growers, and processors of biological materials for classroom and lab use
- Commercial medical labs
- Cosmetics makers
- Food processors
- Makers of agricultural chemicals, including pesticides, growth regulators, fertilizers, and dietary supplements
- Makers of lab equipment and supplies
- Medical device makers
- Petroleum products companies
- Pharmaceutical companies
- Plant and animal breeders and growers
- Public utilities
- Scholarly and textbook publishers
- Seed companies
- Textile and leather makers and users
- Wood growers, harvesters, and processors

The life scientists who work for these employers test for the effects on health of drugs, food additives, dyes, and chemicals; study the effects of construction and energy projects on the environment; strive to improve food production and processing; maintain quality control; and present information to the public. But they are not only researchers and technicians. Many companies put life scientists, especially those without doctorates, in sales, believing that people who understand a product and its uses can sell it more effectively and can communicate customer needs more precisely and usefully to the research staff. They use these scientists in management as well, with the belief that experts in a field are better able to oversee work in that field.

Not surprisingly, the biotechnology industry is the greatest single source of life science jobs. Part of this industry has been around for many years in the form of the pharmaceutical industry, which has long attracted life scientists. Its activities are diverse. It depends utterly on its researchers for new products and continued success, and it gives its scientists practically everything they need in the way of equipment, materials, and technical assistance. It also allows—even urges—its people to collaborate with researchers in other fields and on campus and to publish scholarly papers and books.

Today, however, "biotechnology" means much more than traditional pharmaceuticals. As discussed under "Hot Spots" earlier, it now includes genetic engineering, work with genomes and stem cells, and a great deal more. In the future, genetic engineering may give us the ability to redesign living things—including crop plants, domestic animals, and even human beings—for both aesthetic and functional reasons. As our capabilities grow, biotechnology will provide more and more career opportunities. Modern biotechnology companies offer their life scientists at least as much in the way of financial and other resources as pharmaceutical companies.

Life scientists find most other industries less appealing. The corporations involved are usually smaller and can therefore afford less in the way of resources; moreover, they deal in fewer products and have less potential for future expansion. Yet they should not be ignored; there are industrial positions in virtually every field for life scientists with bachelor's, master's, or doctoral degrees—jobs as researchers, technicians, managers, and salespeople.

CAREERS IN GOVERNMENT

The federal government hires life scientists in every field to work in virtually every area of its operations. Here are some, but by no means all, of the agencies that employ life scientists:

- Centers for Disease Control (CDC)
- Central Intelligence Agency (CIA)
- Department of Agriculture
- Department of Commerce (National Bureau of Standards, National Oceanic and Atmospheric Administration)
- Department of Defense

- Department of Energy
- Department of the Interior (National Park Service, U.S. Fish and Wildlife Service, Bureau of Land Management)
- Department of Labor (Bureau of Labor Statistics, Occupational Safety and Health Administration [OSHA])
- Department of Transportation
- Environmental Protection Agency (EPA)
- Food and Drug Administration (FDA)
- National Aeronautics and Space Administration (NASA)
- National Institutes of Health (NIH)
- National Science Foundation (NSF)
- Smithsonian Institution
- Department of Veterans Affairs (VA)

Some agencies concentrate on matters of health. The missions of NIH and the CDC are disease-related research. The VA does medical research and delivers health care. OSHA monitors the workplace and enforces regulations designed to protect workers' health and safety. The FDA ensures the safety and efficacy of drugs and food additives. The EPA deals in part with environmental effects on health. The Department of the Interior deals with land and wildlife management, among other things, and its state equivalents hire most game wardens.

Relatively few government programs other than those of NSF, NIH, and the Smithsonian deal much with basic biological research. Most direct their efforts to fulfilling missions assigned to them by Congress.

ORGANIZATIONS FOR LIFE SCIENTISTS

All fields of science have their scientific societies. These societies publish journals (which often carry help-wanted ads), maintain informative websites, and hold annual meetings at which their members present papers and talk with one another. They also run job placement services, publish professional directories, provide low-cost insurance, and provide information on education and careers.

Some societies are multidisciplinary. The American Association for the Advancement of Science (AAAS) includes members in the life, earth, physical, and other sciences. It also publishes the journal *Science*, which runs many job ads. Sigma Xi takes individual researchers as its members and publishes *American Scientist*. There are also many state and local academies of science.

Some multidisciplinary societies are restricted to multiple disciplines within a single science; the American Medical Association and the Federation of American Societies for Experimental Biology (FASEB) are prominent examples. Most societies are both smaller and more restricted in their membership. State societies are restricted in geography, if not in fields. The American Association of Anatomists, American Society for Microbiology, American Physiological Society, Society of Systematic Zoology, and many more are restricted in field.

Many societies offer career information in pamphlets and on websites. The most helpful society may be the American Institute of Biological Sciences (AIBS), which publishes the semipopular magazine *Bioscience*, has a great deal of career information available, and (with the AAAS and FASEB) supports the Commission on Professionals in Science and Technology (cpst.org), an excellent source of employment and salary statistics.

Societies and Sources of
Further Information for Careers In the Life Sciences

American Association for the Advancement of Science (AAAS)
1200 New York Avenue, NW
Washington, DC 20005
www.aaas.org

AAAS Science and Technology Policy Fellowships Program
www.fellowships.aaas.org/congressional

American Association of Botanical Gardens and Arboreta
100 West 10th Street, Suite 614
Wilmington, DE 19801
www.aabga.org

American Association of Museums
1575 Eye Street, Fourth Floor
Washington, DC 20002
www.aam-us.org

American Farm Bureau Foundation for Agriculture
225 Touhy Avenue
Park Ridge, IL 60068-5874
www.ageducate.org/careers

American Institute of Biological Sciences (AIBS)
1444 Eye Street, NW, Suite 200
Washington, DC 20005
www.aibs.org/core

American Physiological Society
9650 Rockville Pike
Bethesda, MD 20814-3991
www.the-aps.org

American Society for Biochemistry and Molecular Biology
9650 Rockville Pike
Bethesda, MD 20814-3996
www.asbmb.org/ASBMB/site.nsf/Pages/HomePag

American Society for Microbiology
1752 N Street, NW
Washington, DC 20036
www.asmusa.org

American Society of Agronomy
677 S. Segoe Road
Madison, WI 53711-1086
www.agronomy.org

American Society of Animal Science
111 N. Dunlap Avenue
Savoy, IL 61874
www.asas.org

Botanical Society of America
1725 Neil Avenue
Columbus, OH 43210-1293
www.botany.org

Bureau of Land Management
U.S. Department of the Interior, Room 3619
1849 C Street, NW
Washington, DC 20240
www.blm.gov/nhp

Crop Science Society of America
677 S. Segoe Road
Madison, WI 53711
www.crops.org

Environmental Career Center
100 Bridge Street, Building C
Hampton, VA 23669
www.environmentalcareer.com

Environmental Careers Organization
179 South Street
Boston, MA 02211
www.eco.org

Federation of American Societies for Experimental Biology (FASEB)
9650 Rockville Pike
Bethesda, MD 20814
www.faseb.org

Forest Service, USDA
P.O. Box 96090
Washington, DC 20090-6090
www.fs.fed.us

Institute of Food Technologists
525 W. Van Buren Street, Suite 1000
Chicago, IL 60607
www.ift.org

National Association of Environmental Professionals
P.O. Box 2086
Bowie, MD 20718
www.naep.org

National Association of Science Writers
P.O. Box 890
Hedgesville, WV 25427
www.nasw.org

Natural Resources Conservation Service
   (formerly Soil Conservation Service)
P. O. Box 2890
Washington, DC 20013
www.nrcs.usda.gov

Society for Range Management
445 Union Boulevard, Suite 230
Lakewood, CO 80228
www.rangelands.orgScriptContent/Index.cfm

Society of American Foresters
5400 Grosvenor Lane
Bethesda, MD 20814-2198
www.safnet.org

Soil and Water Conservation Society
7515 Northeast Ankeny Road
Ankeny, IA 50021
www.swcs.org

Soil Science Society of America
677 S. Segoe Road
Madison, WI 53711
www.soils.org

U.S. Department of Agriculture
USDA Careers
Washington, DC 20250
www.usda.gov/da/employ/careers.html

6

CAREERS IN EARTH SCIENCES

Whereas the helping and social sciences deal with human beings and their health and behavior, and the life sciences deal with all living things, the earth sciences deal with the only home of life that we know: Earth. That is, they deal with the environment of life and are in fact a large part of the environmental sciences.

It should thus not be surprising to find that there is some overlap between certain of the earth sciences and the life sciences. This overlap is greatest where the earth sciences address portions of the Earth where living things abound, such as the oceans, lakes, rivers, and soil. There is also overlap between the life sciences and studies of climate and geography, the earth science that focuses on the Earth's surface and the resources it bears. There is very little overlap between the life sciences and those earth sciences that best fit the image that "earth science" first brings to mind: geology and geophysics address the planet's rocks, the movements of continents, the eruptions of volcanoes, and the shudderings of earthquakes.

The U.S. Department of Labor reports that there are about 97,000 environmental scientists and geoscientists, breaking down to 64,000 environmental scientists, 25,000 geoscientists, and 8,000 hydrologists; 27,000 environmental science and protection technicians; and 10,000 geology and petroleum technicians.

Environmental scientists are concerned with air and water pollution, their effects on humans and wildlife, and measures for cleaning up and protecting the environment from human activities. *Hydrologists* focus on the quantity, distribution, circulation, and physical properties of water in lakes, streams, rivers, and underground aquifers. Their work is essential to environmental protection, flood control, and meeting human needs for freshwater.

Geoscientists are known according to their specialties, as geologists, geochemists, geophysicists, geographers, limnologists, climatologists, meteorologists, oceanographers, and so on. We will look at the earth sciences one by one, starting with geography, the very first science most people ever encounter—and for too many the last.

GEOGRAPHY

As taught in elementary and junior high school, geography deals with the nations and regions of the Earth, their lands and waters, peoples and products, imports and exports. It is a social science, a life science, and an earth science. It is, perhaps, the one science that best summarizes, for pedagogic purposes, the entire world and the human species' activities in that world.

As practiced, geography is equally comprehensive, though the emphasis is more practical than pedagogic. *Geographers* strive to explain why and how people live where they do. They study the nature, distribution, and interaction of the many characteristics of the Earth's surface, especially as these pertain to human needs. They are researchers and analysts on campus, in industry, and in government. They teach, consult, and advise. They are planners and administrators of resource management and economic development.

Their tools are climate records, resource inventories, and soil and water analyses. They gather information from maps, aerial photographs, and Earth-surveying satellites. Because they need sophisticated statistics and advanced mathematics to analyze their data and build explanatory models, they need powerful computers.

Economic geographers concentrate on the distribution of a region's economic activities—forestry, agriculture, mining, and manufacturing—and may advise private firms and governments on where best to locate new facilities. *Political geographers* focus on how political entities fit the land, describing and defining natural boundaries such as rivers and mountain ranges for nations, states, and cities. *Urban geographers* restrict their concerns to cities and their surrounding areas; they may advise in such areas as community and industrial development.

Physical geographers emphasize water systems, landforms, vegetation patterns, wildlife distribution, climate, and other physical aspects of the Earth's surface; they contribute to decisions on defense, conservation, agriculture, transportation, marketing, health, and more. *Regional geographers* deal with the physical, political, and economic geography of a region, such as New England or Michigan's Upper Peninsula. To work effectively, they must also understand local language, culture, history, and customs.

Cartographers compile and interpret geographical data, often with the aid of computers, and design and prepare maps. *Medical geographers* deal with the effects of environment (water, air, climate, soil, vegetation) on health. Often concerned with trace elements, such as fluoride or selenium, or with air and water pollution, they work with public health departments and statisticians to determine environmental effects on health and find causes of diseases.

Other specialties include satellite data interpretation, location analysis, conservation, geographical methods and techniques, and agricultural, cultural, historical, population, rural, and social geography.

Many of the nation's geographers spend their days comfortably indoors. Many more work in the field, as members of multidisciplinary research teams. They may travel to remote parts of the world, and they may need considerable adaptability (to adjust to different cultures) and physical stamina.

In 1980, there were about 15,000 geographers, according to the Bureau of Labor Statistics. The *Occupational Outlook Handbook* reports employment in each field but no longer separates geographers from the category of social scientists, which encompassed only 15,000 people in 2000, *not counting* those employed in education (see Chapter 4).

Jobs exist in geography for people with bachelor's, master's, and doctoral degrees. A bachelor's degree is enough to teach geography in the public school system, and it can qualify one for entry-level jobs in government and industry. In 2000, the median annual pay for geographers was $46,690. Geographers with a bachelor's degree but no experience started with the federal government at $21,900 to $27,200 a year in 2001. Future bachelor's geographers can expect intense competition for the relatively few jobs available.

A master's degree qualifies one for community college teaching and aids advancement greatly in industry and government. Specialists in applied areas can expect good job prospects in planning and marketing. In 2001, the federal government paid new master's graduates with no experience $33,300.

A Ph.D. is essential for most teaching and research positions at colleges and universities, as well as for senior positions in government and industry. The pay for geographers with doctorates is much better, starting at $40,200 per year with the federal government.

The job forecast for doctoral geographers is best for industrial and government research and administrative posts. The best chances on campus are for those who have specialized in quantitative research techniques, computer mapping, and natural resource management.

GEOLOGY

The classic portrait of a *geologist* is a rock hound with a pick and hammer in his or her hands. The modern geologist uses the same tools, but also explosives and seismic recorders to chart the layers of rock deep below the surface, deep-drilling rigs to retrieve samples from the depths, and satellite imagery to map terrain. Both the classic and the modern geologist are students of the Earth's crust. They study structure, composition, and history. They want to know what rocks exist where, how they were formed, and how and why they have moved and changed since their formation. They locate mineral deposits, prepare maps, conduct geological surveys, and advise on the suitability of construction sites.

Economic geologists seek minerals and solid fuels. *Petroleum geologists* seek oil and natural gas deposits. *Marine geologists* study the ocean bottoms. *Engineering geologists* concentrate on construction sites for dams, highways, tunnels, and the like. *Mineralogists* classify and analyze minerals and jewels. *Geochemists* work on the chemical processes that have formed and transformed rocks and laid down mineral deposits. *Volcanologists* focus on volcanoes and strive to understand and predict their eruptions. *Geomorphologists* study the forms of the land's surface and the forces of erosion, glaciation, volcanic eruption, and seismic uplift that have shaped those forms. *Paleontologists* are primarily concerned with the traces of past life (fossils) found in the Earth's rocks. *Geochronologists* seek the ages of rocks and landforms by studying the decay of radioactive elements. *Stratigraphers* study the layers (strata) of rock in the Earth's crust in terms of sequence and mineral and fossil content.

Most of the nation's 25,000 geologists and other geoscientists (with thousands more on campus) spend large amounts of time in the field, but they also work in labs and offices. Most work for petroleum, mining, quarrying, and construction firms, and it is in the resource industries that the job prospects of geologists look best. The Bureau of Labor Statistics projects that employment of geologists seems likely to grow through 2010 about as fast as the average for all occupations. Government jobs seem likely to be stagnant, with many jobs being outsourced to private concerns. Corporate employment will depend on the need to comply with environmental laws and on fluctuations in the energy industry. The outlook may improve drastically if resource shortages develop, which may happen before 2010. Current estimates say that the amount of petroleum drawn from the Earth and made available for human use (as gasoline and heating oil, for instance) will peak before that time. Once the peak is past, we can expect the demand for and prices of petroleum products to rise rapidly. There will surely be many job opportunities in the ensuing rush to find and develop more sources of fossil fuels.

In 2000, the median annual earnings of geoscientists were $56,230. New graduates with bachelor's degrees in geology and the geological sciences could start at over $35,000; new master's graduates could start at about $41,000; and new doctorates could start at $57,500. The best salaries were in the petroleum, mining, and mineral industries. In 2001, federal geologists of all levels averaged $70,763.

GEOPHYSICS

Like geologists, *geophysicists* study the physical structure of the Earth, but they range more broadly as well as more deeply. They exploit the planet's electric, magnetic, and gravitational fields to probe the molten core, study and explain the planet's shape, and map past motions of the continents.

Computers and satellites are among their essential tools, as are magnetometers, seismometers, gravimeters, and drilling rigs.

The American Geophysical Union (AGU) classifies as geophysicists both oceanographers and atmospheric scientists (including meteorologists). However, we will treat those specialties separately here. The AGU also claims the study of other planets for its own, but despite the justice of the claim—the same techniques and theories are applicable to all planets, no matter how distant—we will cover the space sciences in Chapter 8.

Like geography and geology, geophysics has numerous subfields or specialties. *Solid earth geophysicists* seek oil and mineral deposits, study earthquakes, and map the planet. *Exploration geophysicists* also seek oil and minerals. Both use seismic techniques (bouncing sound waves off subsurface structures), magnetic techniques (seeking changes in the Earth's magnetic field), and gravimetric techniques (seeking perturbations of the Earth's gravitational field due to underground concentrations or deficiencies of mass).

Seismologists study earthquakes, using the sound waves they emit to find their source and describe the subsurface features that generate them, even to the point of mapping the three-dimensional structure of the Earth's mantle and core. Seismologists also generate their own sound waves to explore for oil and minerals and to analyze the strength and stability of the soil and rock beneath construction sites. *Geodesists* study the planet's size and shape and its gravitational field to increase the precision of maps; they find careful study of perturbations in the orbits of satellites very useful. *Geomagnetists* deal with the Earth's magnetic field. *Paleomagnetists* describe the way that field has changed in past eons; they can do this because the planet's rocks record the direction of the field at the time of their formation. *Petrologists* study the strength, chemical composition, and crystal structure of rocks.

Yet all these subfields of geophysics deal only with pieces of the whole. People who crave the big picture, who want to grasp the planet all at once, can become *tectonophysicists* and deal with the study of plate tectonics. This subfield examines the processes that drive the motions of the planet's crust: seafloor spreading, continental drift, the subduction of crustal slabs in oceanic trenches, the thrusting of slabs into, over, and past each other to fold up mountain ranges and drive volcanoes and earthquakes. Tectonophysicists thus address the strength, elasticity, rigidity, and thermal properties of the Earth's crustal materials, and they share the concerns of petrologists, seismologists, volcanologists, geochemists, geologists, and geo- and paleomagnetists.

In 2001, the federal government's average pay for geophysicists was $79,660. New graduates with bachelor's degrees in the field could start at over $35,000; new master's graduates could start at about $41,000; and new doctorates could start at $57,500.

The job prospects for geophysicists are adequate, according to the Bureau of Labor Statistics, as employment will grow about as fast as average through 2010. However, this field is subject to the same constraints as geology, and the prospects are surely less rosy for the near future. On the other hand, the prospects are bound to improve, as inevitably the present supplies of oil, gas, and minerals will be exhausted and the search for new supplies and substitutes will intensify. Employment may also increase if and when we finally learn how to forecast earthquakes.

HYDROLOGY

Hydrologists study the distribution, flow, and composition of underground and surface waters. Some address problems of water supply, irrigation, erosion, and flood control. A third of all hydrologists work for the federal government. The rest are found in state government, engineering services firms, management, and even public relations. Demand is likely to increase, for there are no signs that the human population (and hence demand for freshwater) is about to stop growing or that people are about to stop putting their homes, cities, and farms in flood zones. Environmental laws and regulations also create a demand for hydrologists as well as environmental scientists.

In 2000, hydrologists earned a median pay of $55,410. In 2001, federal pay averaged $64,810.

OCEANOGRAPHY

The realm of the *oceanographer* covers over two-thirds of the Earth's surface. It is the oceans, rich with food, covering vast deposits of minerals and fossil fuels, birthplace of storms, highway for ships. Here, oceanographers study tides, winds, currents, fish, seaweed, and the sediments, valleys, and mountain ranges of the ocean floor. Their work aids weather prediction, fisheries, resource discovery and retrieval, and national defense. Their tools are ships, aircraft, satellites, drills, nets, dredges, cameras, maps, computers, and even land-based labs.

Biological oceanographers, close kin to marine biologists, deal with the life of the oceans. They study the life cycles, ecology, and migrations of fish and unravel the manifold effects of marine pollution. *Physical oceanographers* concentrate on nonbiological aspects of the seas, such as tides, winds, currents, upwellings, and temperature patterns. *Geological and geophysical oceanographers* study the portion of the Earth's crust that lies beneath the oceans. *Chemical oceanographers* concentrate on the chemical composition of and the chemical reactions in seawater and sea-bottom sediments. *Oceanographic engineers* design and build the tools and instruments for oceanographic research. They also work on undersea construction projects, as in the laying of cables and the building of oil-drilling platforms. *Limnologists* are freshwater "oceanographers."

There are only a few thousand oceanographers in the United States. Over half work on campus, a quarter for the federal government, and the rest for industry. Bachelor-level oceanographers are beginners, technicians, or laboratory assistants. A doctorate is necessary for most high-level positions, especially in research and teaching.

The oceanographer's pay is similar to that of other earth scientists. In 2001, federal oceanographers averaged $71,881 a year. Jobs for oceanographers should grow at about the average rate through the year 2010. Doctoral-level oceanographers will face the best prospects, while oceanographers with lesser degrees may be able to find jobs only as research assistants or technicians.

METEOROLOGY

Atmospheric scientists, or *meteorologists*, are concerned with the phenomena that take place in the Earth's blanket of air, the atmosphere. With the aid of data obtained from satellites, aircraft, and ground stations, they study winds, clouds, temperature patterns, and precipitation. They strive to understand the physical nature of the atmosphere, its motions and processes, and the ways it affects the surface of the planet, perhaps especially those parts occupied by humans. One of their prime concerns is thus the understanding and prediction of weather and climate.

Operational meteorologists specialize in weather forecasting. They use data on atmospheric movement, temperature, humidity, air pressure, and cloud content to make short-term and long-term predictions. Because of the complexity of the atmosphere, they rely greatly on computer models of the atmosphere. Since these models have improved greatly in recent years, so have weather forecasts. Except in special circumstances, however, even the best computer models allow only short-term predictions with great accuracy. One of those special circumstances is El Niño, a warming of the eastern Pacific that can disrupt weather patterns around the globe for months in fairly predictable ways. Most long-term predictions are necessarily imprecise, but as models have improved, so have the predictions.

Physical meteorologists study the physical and chemical properties of the atmosphere. They probe the upper atmosphere with balloons and sounding rockets, fly data-gathering aircraft through clouds and hurricanes, and—from safe distances—study tornadoes. They want to know why clouds and storms form, why rain and snow fall when and where they do, why and how changes in ocean surface temperature affect the weather, and more. Their results are clearly of great value to weather forecasting. Their studies are of great interest to all who worry about sun-induced skin cancer, for it is physical meteorologists who study the loss of the ultraviolet-blocking stratospheric ozone layer due to human-manufactured chlorofluorocarbons (CFCs, also known as freons) and its slow recovery now that CFC manufacture is a thing largely of the past.

Climatologists are interested in long-term weather patterns, or climate. By studying an area's past weather records, they define the area's climate. Changes in past and present patterns—a warming, a cooling, or an increase or decrease in precipitation—then lead them to the causes of climate change, from shifts in the Earth's orbit to changes in the sun's output of heat to volcanic clouds. Climatologists are very useful in land use planning, building design, and the planning of heating and cooling systems. They also help predict the effects of human activities on future climate and are therefore at the center of the debate over global warming, the current warming of the globe resulting from the release of carbon dioxide due to the burning of fossil fuels and the clearing of land.

Most people think of meteorologists in terms of television and radio weather forecasters. However, these people often do little more than report forecasts made by other meteorologists, such as those employed by the National Weather Service (NWS). Of the nation's 6,900 meteorologists (other than college and university faculty), 3,000 work for the federal government (mostly in the NWS, although several hundred civilian meteorologists work for the Department of Defense. (The military employs thousands of its personnel in meteorological work.) The rest work for commercial airlines, weather consulting firms, aerospace firms, and other private enterprises. TV and radio are only the visible tip of the iceberg.

A bachelor's degree is the minimum essential for an entry-level job in weather forecasting. In 2001, bachelor's graduates could start with the federal government at $24,245 or $29,440 per year. Advanced degrees are necessary for research, teaching, and supervisory and administrative positions. The federal government pays a beginning master's graduate $29,440 or $36,606 and a new doctorate $47,039 or $59,661. The average federal meteorologist earned $68,100 in 2001. In 2000, the median pay for all meteorologists was $58,510.

Jobs for meteorologists should grow as fast as the average for all occupations through the year 2010. The best job prospects will be in private industry and for those with advanced degrees.

HOT SPOTS

The hottest areas in the earth sciences at present relate to earthquakes, climate forecasting, and climate change. Tectonophysics, volcanology, and seismology are fields that promise to give us a way to predict earthquakes and volcanic eruptions and hence to escape danger. Atmospheric chemistry deals with both ozone loss (with its threat of skin cancer, cataracts, and crop damage) and climate change. The latter, however, is still more the concern of climatology and long-term weather forecasting. Over the last few decades, the evidence has mounted impressively that carbon dioxide added to the atmosphere by human use of fossil fuels, the making of concrete, and the clearing of land is warming the planet. The 1990s saw several of the warmest years on record, and it seems likely that as the trend continues, floods and droughts will become more common and severe, severe storms will become more numerous, agricultural zones will shift, and the sea level will rise, perhaps enough to inundate crowded coastal communities, such as those in Bangladesh.

The intersection of the earth sciences with the space sciences is also active. There is a growing realization that life on Earth suffered serious setbacks in the past when large comets or asteroids collided with the planet (when an object 10 kilometers in diameter struck the Yucatán coast 65 million years ago, 70 percent of all the species on Earth—including the dinosaurs—were made extinct) and that such collisions will inevitably happen again. Satellites have proved of immense value to weather forecasting and to surveys of the Earth's surface (for mapping, seeking mineral deposits, and appraising human activities such as agriculture, urban spread, and new construction). They have also helped extend the purview of the earth scientists to other planets, as have those few spacecraft that have landed on Mars. By providing comparative data, they have aided the understanding of processes on Earth itself.

CAREERS ON CAMPUS

A smaller percentage of doctoral earth scientists than doctoral life scientists work on campus. Their jobs, however, are similar in that they teach, do research, and earn comparable pay. They may also work in museums and in nearby affiliated or unaffiliated private research outfits. Many academic earth scientists are also consultants to industry and may earn more in this capacity than they earn from their primary employer.

CAREERS IN INDUSTRY

The energy and mining industries dominate private employment of earth scientists, but many others also employ geologists, cartographers, geophysicists, meteorologists, and oceanographers. They rely on these scientists to find fossil fuels and minerals and work out the best techniques for extracting them, to prepare maps, and to forecast weather. Many geographers work for text and map publishers, travel agencies, and insurance companies. Many earth scientists wind up in management and sales positions. The pay tends to be more liberal in industry than on campus or in government.

CAREERS IN GOVERNMENT

The federal government employs earth scientists in the National Oceanic and Atmospheric Administration and its National Weather Service, in the Bureau of Mines and U.S. Geological Survey of the Department of the Interior, in the National Bureau of Standards, in the National Science Foundation, and in the Departments of Defense and Energy. Still others work for NASA, the EPA, and the Departments of Agriculture and Transportation. Their functions were described earlier in this chapter.

Earth scientists can also work as congressional fellows and staff scientists and as lobbyists. In such positions, they work to supply reliable advice to members of Congress. As lobbyists, they may strive to persuade Congress to fund particular energy development or research projects.

ORGANIZATIONS FOR EARTH SCIENTISTS

Like life scientists, earth scientists can belong to numerous professional societies, many of which offer career information and help in finding jobs. The multidisciplinary societies to which earth scientists may belong include the American Association for the Advancement of Science, Sigma Xi, and local and state academies of science. More specialized societies follow shortly.

Job announcements appear regularly in *Science* (AAAS) and in the publications and on the websites of the field's professional societies. The American Geological Institute offers career guides on its website. The American Society of Petroleum Geologists provides links to www.geosciencejobs.com and www.petroleumjobs.com. The Geological Society of America provides numerous useful resources and links, as does the Society of Exploration Geophysicists. The American Meteorological Society offers a thoroughgoing career guide for the atmospheric sciences at www.ametsoc.org /AMS/AtmosCareers/index.html.

Societies and Sources of Further Information for Careers in the Earth Sciences

American Geological Institute
4220 King Street
Alexandria, VA 22302-1502
www.agiweb.org

American Geophysical Union
2000 Florida Avenue, NW
Washington, DC 20009
www.agu.org

American Meteorological Society
45 Beacon Street
Boston, MA 02108
www.ametsoc.org/AMS

American Society of Petroleum Geologists
P.O. Box 979
Tulsa, OK 74101
www.aapg.org

Association of American Geographers
1710 16th Street, NW
Washington, DC 20009-3198
www.aag.org

Geological Society of America
P.O. Box 9140
3300 Penrose Place
Boulder, CO 80301-9140
www.geosociety.org

Marine Technology Society
5565 Sterrett Place, #108
Columbia, MD 21044
www.mtsociety.org

Society of Exploration Geophysicists
8801 South Yale
Tulsa, OK 74137-2740
www.seg.org

CHAPTER 7

CAREERS IN PHYSICAL SCIENCES

The physical sciences are chemistry, physics, and their offspring, materials science. Putting things as simply as possible, chemistry is the study of the interactions of atoms and molecules, while physics is the study of the behavior of single atoms and their component pieces, of large assemblages of matter—crystals and bricks, liquids and gases, planets and stars—and of energy. Materials science deals with surfaces, catalysts, alloys, crystals, and production techniques for such devices as the integrated circuit chips that make personal computers, PDAs, cell phones, and many other modern devices possible.

The physical sciences thus deal with neither life nor the environment but with the components of both. Their domain is matter in all its forms, energy, and the interactions of the two. They generate knowledge crucial to our understanding of the universe and essential to all other fields of science. They are at the roots of technology and engineering, and their fruits saturate our daily lives.

Physical scientists work in both basic and applied research. Relatively few teach on campus. Most work for industry, in research and development. Average incomes are thus high, and there are jobs for people with all levels of education, even for brand-new high school graduates.

CHEMISTRY

Chemistry is the science of substances, the study of atoms and molecules, elements and compounds. *Chemists* break matter down to learn its components, and they put components together to make new substances. They study the ways in which the components go together in chemical reactions and the ways in which they can fall apart again. They have invented synthetic materials, such as nylon, polyethylene, and other plastics; additives to preserve food and enhance lubricants; methods to convert the useless gunk that is raw petroleum into free-flowing gasoline; and much, much more. They work in the textile, food, energy, electronics, glass, paper, packaging, machinery, cosmetics, paint, drug, and chemical industries, to name a few. They are almost as ubiquitous as life scientists, and they may be more essential to civilization as we know it.

Most of the nation's 92,000 chemists and materials scientists work in industry, many in research and development and the rest in production, quality control, management, sales, and even finance. They may also work in advertising, public relations, environmental protection, and industrial safety and health departments. They may be writers, editors, patent agents, and attorneys.

Many chemists work in colleges and universities. An equal number work for federal, state, and local governments. Government chemists also do R&D work, but many are in safety, health, and environmental protection as inspectors and regulators. On campus, chemists concentrate on teaching and research.

Like most sciences, chemistry can be broken into several subfields. The major ones are biochemistry, physical chemistry, organic chemistry, inorganic chemistry, and analytical chemistry. *Biochemists* deal with the chemistry of living things—with proteins, fats, starches, DNA, and drugs (see Chapter 5).

Physical chemists are concerned with the physical properties of matter. They strive to describe, in rigorous mathematical terms, the conversion of solid to liquid and liquid to gas (and vice versa). They study the statistics of molecular interactions, and their work on combustion and on the plasmas ("gases" of ions) that will one day provide fusion power contributes to the improvement of existing energy sources and the development of new ones.

Organic chemists focus on carbon-containing (organic) compounds, such as those produced by living organisms. They thus work in the petroleum, coal, wood products, plastics, textiles, and food industries. They devise new synthetic materials and new production processes for old materials. They convert one material to another—such as turning the hydrocarbons in petroleum and coal into useful, clean fuels or turning the waste products of the paper industry into feedstocks for chemical and plastics plants. They also study the ways in which carbon combines with other substances.

Inorganic chemists focus on non-carbon-containing compounds. They find employment in the mining industries, where ores must be broken down to retrieve pure metals and other substances. They work in the electronics industry, devising materials and methods for the construction of solid-state electronic components such as integrated circuits. They devise inorganic catalysts for both organic and inorganic reactions, as for the production of ammonia (for fertilizer) and methane (synthetic natural gas), for the liquefaction and gasification of coal, and for the removal of pollutants from automobile and factory exhausts.

Analytical chemists analyze. Using chemical tests, gas chromatographs, spectroscopes, and other sophisticated equipment, they seek the exact composition of substances. They are crucial to industrial quality control, for they check the purity of raw materials and finished products. Often, they are troubleshooters; a textile plant's color or dye chemist, faced with a problem such as the failure of a dye to stick to a fabric, may analyze drying agents, dyes, and other materials to find a solution.

Analytical chemists are also important in government, for they monitor air and water pollution and food and drug purity. Some work as *forensic chemists* for police departments and the FBI. They develop evidence in criminal cases by analyzing samples of blood, saliva, and other body fluids, as well as soils, fibers, and other substances. Their work intersects with the life sciences, most famously in recent years with the use of DNA in blood, semen, and even hair to match evidence to suspects; in a gratifyingly large number of cases, the result has been the exoneration of suspects and their release from prison, even from death row.

It is possible to classify chemists in narrower terms. Job descriptions often name forensic, food, color, dye, paper, and petroleum chemists; environmental chemists; development chemists; and quality control or assurance chemists. However, the broader classification by function and approach instead of by job may be more useful to anyone who is looking for a career.

Chemists generally work on a relatively small scale, using milligrams or grams of material in labs fitted with test tubes, beakers, distillation columns, flasks, stirrers, heaters, lasers, and electronic equipment. *Chemical engineers*, whose job is to turn laboratory processes into industrial production, work on a much larger scale, with ton lots of raw material and acres of vats and pipes. We will consider them in more detail in Chapter 9.

Chemists with doctoral degrees are qualified for college and university teaching and research positions and for industrial and government research and administration posts. A master's degree is enough for many jobs in applied research and for some college and community college teaching positions. A bachelor's degree will do for many beginning jobs as research assistant, product tester or analyst, or technical sales or service representative.

According to the U.S. Department of Labor, the job prospects for chemists will be best in the drug manufacturing, research and development, and testing services. Overall, employment is expected to expand about as fast as the average for all occupations through the year 2010.

Pay is and will continue to be good. In 2000, the median pay for chemists was just over $50,000. The American Chemical Society reports that in 2000, chemists holding a bachelor's degree averaged $55,000 per year, those with a master's degree averaged $65,000, and doctorates averaged $82,200. Starting salaries were, of course, lower, averaging $33,500 for bachelor's graduates, $44,100 for master's graduates, and $64,500 for new doctorates. Federal pay ran somewhat lower, with federal chemists averaging $70,435 in 2001. Pay was best in private industry and poorest on campus.

PHYSICS

Physicists consider themselves the most fundamental of scientists, for they are the ones who work out the basic laws of nature. They study the nature and behavior of atoms and their components (electrons, protons, and neutrons) and of the components of electrons, protons, and neutrons (kaons, pions, muons, and quarks, among others). They study what happens when atoms and subatomic particles break down and assemble, how they react to collisions with each other and to electromagnetic radiation.

They study the flow of electrons in solids, of light in space, and of water in pipes. They apply the laws of classical mechanics to the study of how objects fall, orbit, and bang together; the laws of quantum mechanics to the study of subatomic particles; and Einstein's theory of relativity to the study of objects at great distances in space and at very high speed. Always, they use mathematics to understand, explain, and predict; their theories are equations. Almost always, they apply their predictions and theories to other fields—to chemistry, biology, geophysics, and engineering; to communications, transportation, electronics, and health.

In 2000, some 9,000 physicists were employed in the United States, not counting those on college and university faculty. About 35 percent of non-faculty physicists work for the federal government, mostly in the Department of Defense, with some in the National Aeronautics and Space Administration and the Departments of Energy and Commerce.

Some physicists work in health-related fields. *Biophysicists* apply the laws of physics to biological systems, studying vision, hearing, nerve action, blood flow, and even the behavior of DNA. *Health physicists* are concerned with the effects of radiation and radioactive materials on biological systems. *Medical physicists* study the use of ionizing (nuclear, X-ray) and thermal radiation in diagnosis and treatment, methods of recording and interpreting the electrical activity of the brain and heart, and the use of high-frequency sound. They design, build, and use ultrasound, CAT (computerized axial tomography), PET (positron-emission tomography), and MRI (magnetic resonance imaging) scanners that construct images of the interior of the body.

The more traditional varieties of physicists steer clear of biology. *Solid-state physicists* study metals, alloys, ceramics, semiconductors, and insulators, contributing most to metallurgy, engineering, and electronics. *Nuclear physicists* focus on the interior of the atom with cyclotrons and larger particle accelerators. They are responsible for bombs, power plants, and the radioactive tracers invaluable in medical diagnosis. *Elementary particle physicists* extend the nuclear physicist's purview to the components of the components of the atom. The applications of these subcomponents so far are few, but they promise a unified view of the universe and perhaps new energy sources, transportation methods, and more. *Atomic, molecular,* and *electron physicists* study how electrons and nuclei interact, how atoms combine as molecules, and how the electrons of atoms and molecules respond to radiation. They help chemists understand chemical reactions, and they have birthed the technique of spectroscopy, whereby tiny amounts of substances can be identified by the light they give off when heated.

Optical physicists study light and design lenses, fiber optics, and lasers. *Acoustical physicists* focus on sound and contribute to the design of microphones, speakers, CD players, and hearing aids. *Fluid physicists* deal with the flow of liquids and gases and help design cars, jet engines, and plumbing systems. *Plasma physicists* study electrically charged fluids, or plasmas; many are involved in the attempt to make fusion energy work. *Planetary physicists* are geophysicists under another name that lets them study other worlds as well as Earth. *Space physicists* study the regions beyond the atmosphere; *astrophysicists* and *cosmologists* study stars and the universe. With planetary physicists, they are all space scientists, whom we will discuss in Chapter 8.

Any physicist can be either an experimentalist or a theoretician. The theoreticians almost invariably have a doctorate. So do most of the experimentalists, since the doctorate is essential for college and university teaching and research, for upper-level research positions in government and industry, and for higher administrative positions. Physicists with a master's degree can find some research (particularly in private industry) and teaching positions. Those with only a bachelor's degree can get into applied research and development or find jobs as research assistants or technicians. Many bachelor's graduates work in design, administration, and engineering.

In 2000, physicists enjoyed a median pay of $83,310. According to the American Institute of Physics, the median salary of its Ph.D. members in that year was $78,000; of its master's degree members, $63,800; and of its bachelor's degree members, $60,000. Federal government physicists averaged $86,799 in 2001.

Because defense expenditures are expected to increase for the next few years, the employment of physicists should increase about as fast as the average for all occupations through the year 2010. Increased expenditures by the Department of Homeland Security may improve that prospect.

MATERIALS SCIENCE

Materials scientists focus heavily on the properties of the substances people use in various devices. Thus, materials science has strong components of chemistry and physics. Physicists who work in this area may emphasize the manipulation of electronic materials, as in the etching of circuits on silicon chips with ultraviolet, X-ray, and electron beams. They also develop new construction materials, components for batteries and fuel cells, and more. Chemists develop polymers for many purposes, from food wrappers to the latest in organic electronics.

Materials scientists also include crystallographers, who study the way atoms pack together in crystalline and noncrystalline (amorphous) solids and in thin films, membranes, fibers, glasses, liquids, and gases. Their work contributes to the electronics industry, to the conversion of sunlight to electricity with photovoltaic cells, to the understanding of how radiation affects the structural materials of nuclear reactors, and to improving the shelf life and effectiveness of drugs.

Other materials scientists work in the area of metallurgy, studying metal alloys and striving to improve their strength and other properties. Still others study how atoms and molecules attach to surfaces, and their work feeds directly into the study of catalysts. Some materials scientists spend their lives designing new catalysts. They may design novel molecules with very specific shapes to catalyze specific industrial reactions; the catalysts they produce may be either organic or inorganic.

Because materials scientists are either physicists or chemists, they are paid on the same scales. Their job prospects, however, are somewhat better, for materials science is a growing field. New techniques are available; there is a strong need for improved catalysts, and the electronics industry is straining for technological advances.

HOT SPOTS

Chemistry, physics, and materials science are closely associated with the development of new technologies. Even in an era that promises to pay a great deal of attention to biotechnology, there is and will remain the Internet, whose second generation is already taking form, with demands for better fiber-optic cables, more capacious hard drives, and so on. There are laptop computers, personal digital assistants (PDAs), and cell phones, all creating a demand for wireless connections to the world's communications networks and the Internet as well as for compact energy storage devices. And nanotechnology promises a host of microscopic devices with near-miraculous capabilities.

Energy research remains of vital concern, and the conversion of sunlight to electricity is now very near economic practicality. Some physical science researchers are striving to construct artificial organs that the human body will tolerate for long periods of time. Others are developing new and exceedingly sensitive sensors for pollutants, contaminants, toxins, and other substances by combining biological molecules (enzymes) or cells with electronics.

Environmental work is important in other ways as well. Chemists are crucial to the cleanup of contaminated sites, and the end of the Cold War has resulted in the dismantling of much of the nuclear armament that for so long hung as a threat over the world's collective head. Chemists are also involved in cleaning up after terrorist attacks and developing defenses against such attacks. Physicists are behind the scanners now found at every airport and many public buildings.

On a more abstract level, research continues in the areas of elementary particle physics and cosmology, the ultimately small and the ultimately large. The current models of particle accelerators—underground circular tunnels miles in circumference—are revealing the finest structure of matter. The cosmologists are studying the beginning and the end of our universe and sketching theories that suggest the existence of many more universes besides our own. Many of their theories are based on the results of experiments in elementary particle physics. We will say a little more about the work of cosmologists in Chapter 8.

CAREERS ON CAMPUS

Like life and earth scientists, physical scientists teach and do research at universities and colleges and teach without the research at community colleges. They may also teach at the high school level.

As the number of college and university faculty continues to grow (by 23 percent between 2000 and 2010), the number of campus positions for physical scientists is bound to increase. After years of intense competition for available positions, the number of physics doctorates granted each year has begun to drop, which may ease competition a little. In chemistry, as in the life sciences, many new doctorates will spend a year or two in the post-doctoral holding pattern.

CAREERS IN INDUSTRY

While most physicists work on campus, by far most chemists and materials scientists work in industry. They work in research and development and in production, in quality control and in marketing, and in many other positions. Physicists in industry occupy a similar range of jobs. Almost always, they serve the corporate goals of new products, productivity, efficiency, and profit. If they serve these goals well, physical scientists can easily wind up in managerial posts.

CAREERS IN GOVERNMENT

The federal government's physical scientists work for the Departments of Energy, Defense, Homeland Security, Interior, Justice, Commerce, Agriculture, and Health and Human Services and for the National Bureau of Standards, National Institutes of Health, National Science Foundation, Smithsonian Institution, National Aeronautics and Space Administration, Environmental Protection Agency, Patent Office, Food and Drug Administration, and Occupational Safety and Health Administration. They are everywhere, as analysts, managers, administrators, inspectors, regulators, and congressional staffers. They are even a large number of lobbyists. They are also, of course, researchers, working on problems related to defense and energy, among others.

ORGANIZATIONS FOR PHYSICAL SCIENTISTS

Physical scientists can belong to the American Association for the Advancement of Science, Sigma Xi, and more specialized societies. For prospective physicists, career information is available from the American Institute of

Physics. More general information is available in the magazines *Physics Today* and *Bulletin of the Atomic Scientists.*

The big society for chemists is the American Chemical Society. It offers a wealth of career information, runs an Employment Clearing House and an Employment Aids Office, and publishes the weekly *Chemical and Engineering News.* It also publishes *Student Affiliate Newsletter,* which contains much career information, as well as a variety of journals.

Societies and Sources of Further Information for Careers in the Physical Sciences

American Association of Physicists in Medicine
One Physics Ellipse
College Park, MD 20740-3843
www.aapm.org

American Association of Physics Teachers
One Physics Ellipse
College Park, MD 20740-3843
www.aapt.org

American Chemical Society
1155 16th Street, NW
Washington, DC 20036
www.chemistry.org/portal/chemistry

American Chemistry Council
1300 Wilson Boulevard
Arlington, VA 22209
www.americanchemistry.com

American Institute of Chemical Engineers
3 Park Avenue
New York, NY 10016-5991
www.aiche.org

American Institute of Physics
One Physics Ellipse
College Park, MD 20740-3843
www.aip.org

American Physical Society
One Physics Ellipse
College Park, MD 20740-3843
www.aps.org

Federation of Materials Societies
910 17th Street, NW, Suite 800
Washington, DC 20006
www.materialsocieties.org

Materials Research Society
506 Keystone Drive
Warrendale, PA 15086-7573
www.mrs.org

National Organization for the Professional Advancement of
    Black Chemists and Chemical Engineers
P.O. Box 77040
Washington, DC 20013
www.nobcche.org

National Society of Black Physicists
6704G Lee Highway
Arlington, VA 22205
www.nsbp.org

CHAPTER

8

CAREERS IN SPACE SCIENCES

The Labor Department's *Occupational Outlook Handbook* lists only two space science careers: astronomer and aerospace engineer. We will consider the latter in Chapter 9, with all the other engineers. The former has its place in this chapter. But is it truly alone? Is there really only one space science that is not a field of engineering?

Of course not. The space sciences are all those sciences and subfields that study or exploit some aspect of the space environment. Meteorologists are space scientists when they help design and launch and then use weather satellites and when they study the effects of solar activity on terrestrial weather. Climatologists are space scientists when they seek to understand the processes that drive climate change by studying the climates of other worlds. So are geographers when they design, launch, and use Earth-surveying satellites. So are geologists and geophysicists when they turn their eyes to other planets (as do planetologists) with the aid of flyby, orbiting, and landing spacecraft. So are life scientists when they focus on how space affects terrestrial organisms or on the prospects for extraterrestrial biology. So are chemists, metallurgists, biochemists, and others who wish to use the special qualities of the space environment (weightlessness, vacuum, and so on) in research and manufacturing.

The space sciences thus have something for scientists of every description. Yet space is not only for scientists. It is for all the human beings crowded together on this planet Earth, exposed as we are to drought, flood, crop failures, and resource shortages. Relatively few of us will ever be able to leave this planet for other worlds or for the space habitats that may be built within the next century, but all of us can and will benefit from the virtually endless supplies of energy and raw materials available in space. We need only build the satellites that can trap the bountiful sunlight that shines twenty-four hours a day in orbit and convert it to electricity for use on Earth. We need only establish bases and mines on the moon to be able to bring home and process asteroids and comets. We need only move the polluting industries into orbit. Earth's air and water will then be clean, and all Earth's billions will be able to enjoy a standard of living now known to only a few.

This prescription sounds like science fiction. But serious plans for just such grandiose developments have been on the drawing boards for years, and the admittedly colossal expense is less of an obstacle than one might think. So far we have used space mostly as a vantage point from which satellites can watch for storms, seek mineral deposits, provide cartographic data, appraise crops, and tell navigators on ships and planes their positions. However, these simple uses of space have already repaid tenfold every dollar spent on space programs. There is no reason to think that the benefit-to-cost ratio of further space programs will be any worse.

But this science fiction future will not come tomorrow. It is a long-term dream that, because the necessary initial investment is so large, depends on a thriving national and international economy. It also depends on the continued collection of information. What resources are available on the moon? We must spend more time there, prospecting from permanent bases. What resources are available in asteroids and comets? We must visit them and see. How safe is life in space? We must try it and see, with orbiting space stations, moon bases, and trips to the other planets of our solar system.

Other work in the space sciences also has its relevance to life on Earth. *Solar and stellar physicists* study how stars produce vast outpourings of energy from thermonuclear fusion reactions, which may provide the key to safe, cheap, workable fusion reactors on Earth. *Planetologists*—the geologists, geochemists, and geophysicists of space—study how other planets have formed and evolved; by giving us a basis for comparison, they help us understand earthquakes, plate tectonics, volcanoes, and mineral deposits.

Atmospheric scientists study the gaseous cloaks, clouds, and storms of other worlds; they help us understand the dynamics of earthly weather.

We have said that careers in science are dedicated to human survival. This may be nowhere truer than in the space sciences, for while these fields contribute to many human needs, they also offer an invaluable insurance policy. Life on a planet is vulnerable, for planets can be hit by massive bodies of rock, such as the asteroid or comet that apparently smashed into Earth some 65 million years ago, extinguishing the dinosaurs and myriad other life-forms and marking the end of the Cretaceous period. That same type of disaster can happen again. It is bound to, eventually. And the human species can have little protection as long as it remains confined to the surface of a single planet (NASA held a "Workshop on Scientific Requirements for Mitigation of Hazardous Comets and Asteroids" in September 2002; www.noao.edu/meetings/mitigation/report.html). But if part of the species can move to space stations, space habitats, and other worlds, then the species as a whole will be able to survive almost anything the universe can throw at it. Some humans will be able to survive asteroid impacts, ice ages, solar flares—even planetary thermonuclear war.

But first we must escape the naked surface of this round ball of rock we call home. It is the space sciences that will help us do that. It is the space sciences that will get our species off its planetary eight ball.

Sadly, the U.S. space program has lost an enormous amount of momentum. The process began even as American astronauts were walking on the moon, when then-president Nixon slashed the program's funds. The program managed to continue, however, until it could launch the first reusable spacecraft, the space shuttle, and with it an enormous cargo of hopes for the future. Those hopes were sorely threatened when the *Challenger* shuttle blew up and the space program shut down for almost three years. They were threatened once more when the Hubble Space Telescope turned out to have a defective mirror that could produce at best fuzzy images of the deeps of space. They were threatened yet again when the long-awaited space station's construction estimates grew so huge that Congress forced redesigns to save money. The shuttles did begin to fly again, the Hubble was repaired, and the space station was built. But at this writing, the space program is struggling to cope with the destruction of the *Columbia* on its return from orbit February 1, 2003.

We are as far as we ever were from building space habitats or moon bases or visiting Mars or turning *Star Trek* into reality, but we do still have a space program, a toehold on the science fiction future. And meanwhile, those weather and communications and Earth-surveying satellites are still being launched, for they have proved invaluable to modern civilization. Current space program news is available at www.nasa.gov.

ASTRONOMY

The oldest of the space sciences—and the only one we will treat purely as a space science here—is astronomy. It is what first leaps to mind when one thinks of "space science." Most of the other space sciences find their origins in astronomy. The builders of satellites and spacecraft take places beside the builders of telescopes. Earth's weather sidles up beside that of Jupiter and Mars and Venus. The work of geophysicists and planetologists, astrophysicists and plasma physicists, and cosmologists and particle physicists all depends to some extent on astronomy.

Traditionally, the *astronomer* has looked through telescopes to study the stars—their movements, changes, types, and distributions—and the planets and their satellites (moons). Today, very few astronomers actually apply eye to telescope. Modern astronomical equipment is electronic, controlled by computers and receiving the light of the stars and planets with detectors far more efficient than either the human eye or photographic film. The Hubble Space Telescope's unprecedentedly sharp images are totally electronic. Some telescopes observe the stars in wavelengths of light that the human eye cannot see at all. There are infrared telescopes, radio telescopes, and even ultraviolet, X-ray, and gamma ray telescopes (which work only in orbit, above the atmosphere).

Modern astronomers also exploit spacecraft. With the *Mariner, Viking, Odyssey,* and *Global Surveyor* missions, they have photographed the surface of Mars, analyzed actual samples of the Martian surface, and mapped the distribution of water. With the *Pioneer, Voyager,* and *Galileo* spacecraft, they have photographed the clouds and moons of Jupiter and the rings of Saturn and Uranus and gained reams of information to confound and delight the theorists. They have surveyed the fluxes of radiation, magnetic fields, and particles from Mercury to beyond Uranus. They have even probed the atmosphere and surface of Venus. They listen for hints of other radio-using civilizations. And more missions are under way (*Cassini-Huygens* will reach Saturn in 2004 and put a lander on Saturn's moon Titan in 2005) or pending (rovers and sample-return missions for Mars).

With optical and radio telescopes, *solar astronomers* study the sun, its radiations, its magnetic fields, and its vast eruptions of plasma. Using tanks of cleaning fluid deep in empty mines, they count neutrinos to study the processes of thermonuclear fusion that fuel the sun. With spacecraft, they sample and plot the solar wind, the flood of particles sleeting outward from the sun. They photograph and chart sunspots. They chase eclipses with aircraft to gain glimpses of the sun's corona.

Our sun is the nearest star, and solar astronomy is the close-at-hand subfield of astrophysics. *Astrophysicists* strive to understand how stars function and change as they age, how they form from clouds of dust and gas, and how they degenerate into white dwarfs, neutron stars, and black holes. They theorize about the unobservable and the yet unknown, trying to see through cryptic observations to the nature and characteristics of black holes and quasars.

Cosmologists probe the limits of the observable universe, over 10 billion light-years away from Earth, plot the distribution of galaxies and clusters of galaxies, and devise theories of how the universe, some 10 to 15 billion years ago, exploded from a pointlike mass. They are theorists, and they are kin to the particle physicists, who believe that at its beginning, the universe was nothing but subatomic particles and energy. Some theorists suggest that our universe is but a bubble in some vaster cosmos that we can never know.

According to the American Astronomical Society, about 6,000 astronomers are employed in North America. Fifty-five percent work as university and college faculty or at university-affiliated observatories and laboratories. The rest hold jobs with the Department of Defense, NASA, and industry. Very few ever spend more than a few weeks a year making observations with telescopes or other instruments. The rest of the time they spend teaching, writing and reading research proposals, keeping up with their field, attending scientific meetings, designing new observational instruments, and analyzing their own and others' observations. Many devote their time almost wholly to theories and mathematical models, working intimately with computers. Some are applied mathematicians, using computers and observations of the sun, moon, and planets to calculate tide tables and the orbits of both natural and artificial satellites.

Most jobs in astronomy require a doctorate in the field. Lesser degrees qualify one only for jobs as an assistant to a Ph.D. astronomer, a data processor, an instrument builder or operator, or perhaps a writer or editor in the field. However, many of these jobs are filled by Ph.D. astronomers. Competition for astronomical positions is keen, partly because the equipment necessary for observations—telescopes and spacecraft—is so expensive that it is in very limited supply and offers few people the chance to use it. Competition is also keen because the field is small and few replacements are needed. Still, employment for astronomers is expected to grow about as fast as the average for all occupations through 2010.

The pay is good. In 2000, astronomers averaged $74,510. In 2001, astronomers and other space scientists employed by the federal government averaged $89,734. Astronomers on campus make about the same as physicists.

HOT SPOTS

It has been many years since the heyday of planetary exploration, when *Apollo* astronauts visited the moon and *Viking* spacecraft landed on Mars, when *Pioneers* and *Voyagers* first photographed the outer worlds. But in the 1990s, several important expeditions were launched to study Mars, Jupiter, Saturn, the sun, and of course Earth itself. (See www. jpl.nasa.gov/ missions/index.cfm for a list of currently active missions. Future missions are cited at jpl.nasa.gov/missions/future_missions.cfm. Proposed missions —including one designed to find Earth-like planets orbiting other stars— are at www.jpl.nasa.gov/missions/proposed_missions.cfm.)

The Hubble Space Telescope is a grand success story. Since its repair by shuttle-borne astronauts, it has supplied an endless suite of breathtaking images of the most distant reaches of the cosmos. Improvements in ground-based telescopes have come close to matching it. Radio telescopes have collected clues to the origin and destiny of the universe. X-ray, gamma ray, infrared, and ultraviolet telescopes have also delivered a wealth of information, and there really does seem no end in sight.

Plans to replace the aging space shuttle fleet have gained urgency since the loss of the *Columbia*. The Advanced Space Transportation Program at NASA's Marshall Space Flight Center in Huntsville, Alabama, notes (at www1.msfc.nasa.gov/NEWSROOM/background/facts/astp.html):

> Dramatic improvements are required to make space transportation safer and more affordable. . . . The Advanced Space Transportation Program [ASTP] is developing technologies that target a 100-fold reduction in the cost of getting to space by 2025, lowering the price tag to $100 per pound. . . . These advanced technologies would move space transportation closer to an airline style of operations with horizontal takeoffs and landings, quick turnaround times and small ground support crews.
>
> This third generation of launch vehicles . . . depends on a wide variety of cutting-edge technologies, such as advanced propellants that pack more energy into smaller tanks and result in smaller launch vehicles. Advanced thermal protection systems also will be necessary for future launch vehicles because they will fly faster through the atmosphere, resulting in higher structural heating than today's vehicles.
>
> Another emerging technology—intelligent vehicle health management systems—could allow the launch vehicle to determine its own health without human inspection. Sensors embedded in the vehicle could send signals to determine if any damage occurs during flight. Upon landing, the vehicle's onboard computer could download the vehicle's health status to a ground controller's laptop computer, recommend specific maintenance points or tell the launch site it's ready for the next launch.

If the ASTP succeeds, the future will be wide open for the space sciences. It may even be open enough to warrant choosing a career in the space sciences in anticipation of a future explosion of space science activity.

CAREERS ON CAMPUS

Fifty-five percent of the nation's astronomers work for colleges, universities, or academically affiliated observatories, where they spend most of their time in teaching and research. One in five academic astronomers is a research associate, not faculty but staff. These jobs do not offer tenure and are supposedly short-term, but some astronomers have held them for long periods. Postdoctoral positions also exist.

Science museums and planetariums employ a few astronomers blessed with a performer's flair for popularizing their field and reaching the public. The pay matches that of astronomers on campus, and many of the relatively few people in these jobs are very satisfied with their work.

CAREERS IN INDUSTRY

In the private sector, a few astronomers find work with scientific supply houses and astronomical magazines, such as *Sky and Telescope*. More apply their training in computers, electronics, equipment design, and data analysis to nonastronomical research, for the astronomer's training is general enough and technical enough to open up many satisfying, challenging careers. Still more work for aerospace companies as spacecraft designers and operators, planners, and managers or for companies that do space-related research on contract for government and other companies.

Nonastronomer space scientists work for satellite communications companies, energy companies, and companies that interpret and use the data produced by Earth-surveying satellites. Eventually, industry is likely to move into space more vigorously, pursuing resources on the moon and elsewhere, building solar power satellites and dwelling places, and setting up manufacturing facilities in orbit. For the present, however, most space science jobs will lie on campus and with the government.

CAREERS IN GOVERNMENT

A very few space scientists—mostly ex-astronauts with degrees in astronomy, physics, and engineering—have become senators and representatives.

But they are hardly representative of the 1,000 or so astronomers and other space scientists employed by the federal government in NASA or the Defense Department's U.S. Naval Observatory and U.S. Naval Research Laboratory. Some government astronomers are involved in maintaining and improving navigation systems, both with traditional ephemerides (tables and charts of moon, sun, and star positions) and with satellite beacons and tide tables. Some other space scientists work in meteorology and Earth resources surveying. Many astronomers and other space scientists work as researchers, planners, and managers in the space and defense programs.

The government's space activities are dominated by the Department of Defense and NASA. NASA's proposed 2004 budget for science and technology R&D is just over $9 billion ($4 billion for space science, $1.5 billion for earth science, $2.6 billion for aerospace technology, and $973 million for biological and physical research). The Department of Defense proposed 2004 budget for science and technology R&D is only about $5 billion, and that includes much more than space science.

ORGANIZATIONS FOR SPACE SCIENTISTS

Space scientists may belong to many organizations besides the multidisciplinary standbys (AAAS and Sigma Xi) and many of the organizations for physical and earth scientists. NASA provides career information at www.nasa.gov/about/career/index.html.

The American Astronomical Society publishes several journals and a bimonthly newsletter, provides career information, and runs an online Job Register.

The American Institute of Aeronautics and Astronautics (AIAA) "is the largest professional technical society, principal voice, and information resource devoted to the progress of engineering and science in aviation and space. AIAA's mission is to advance the arts, sciences, and technology of aerospace, and to nurture and promote the professionalism of those engaged in these pursuits. AIAA seeks to meet the professional needs and interests of members as well as to improve public understanding of the profession and its contributions. AIAA provides other resources to foster careers in aerospace, including Career Opportunities advertisements in its flagship magazine, *Aerospace America*."

The American Astronautical Society is dedicated to the advancement of space science and exploration. It publishes books, a journal, and a bimonthly magazine, *The Space Times*. Among many other organizations are the Aerospace Industries Association (www.aia-aerospace.org/index .cfm), the International Astronautical Federation (www.iafastro.com), and the Aerospace Medical Association (www.asma.org). All are primarily for professionals in the space sciences, but amateurs who care about the space sciences and wish to encourage them may also join.

There are also many organizations that are primarily for amateurs and enthusiasts but count many professionals among their members. The most active of these groups is the National Space Society, one portion of which, the L-5 Society, was organized to encourage the building of space colonies and sworn not to disband until it can hold its final meeting on a space colony. It promotes a vigorous U.S. space program and public awareness of the importance of space development. Their internship program gives students a chance to work with them in Washington, DC.

Societies and Sources of Further Information for Careers In the Space Sciences

American Astronautical Society
6352 Rolling Mill Place, Suite #102
Springfield, VA 22152-2354
www.astronautical.org

American Astronomical Society
2000 Florida Avenue, NW, Suite 400
Washington, DC 20009-1231
www.aas.org

American Institute of Aeronautics and Astronautics
1801 Alexander Bell Drive, Suite 500
Reston, VA 20191-4344
www.aiaa.org

Astronomical Society of the Pacific
390 Ashton Avenue
San Francisco, CA 94112
www.astrosociety.org

National Space Society
600 Pennsylvania Avenue, SE, Suite 201
Washington, DC 20003
www.nss.org

CHAPTER

9

CAREERS IN ENGINEERING

The engineering sciences include architecture, landscape architecture, and surveying, as well as aerospace, agricultural, biomedical, chemical, civil, computer hardware, electrical and electronics, environmental, industrial, materials, mechanical, mining and geological, nuclear, and petroleum engineering. Each field may have subdivisions. Civil engineers, for instance, may be structural or highway engineers. Materials engineers may be ceramic, metallurgical, or polymer engineers.

Engineering is often close kin to the life, earth, physical, and space sciences. The main difference is that the engineer is even more interested in specific, useful answers to problems than the applied researcher. Engineers are designers and builders of mechanical, electronic, and—most recently — biological devices. They plan factories to ease the task of production. They design and supervise mines to cope with local geological problems, find ore, and maintain safety. They seek the best ways to extract oil from the ground.

As a group, engineers are quite well paid. Because demand is also high, few engineers go on to obtain degrees beyond the bachelor's. This is partly because teaching jobs simply cannot compete with industrial pay scales. New bachelor's graduates often see little reason to grind away at a higher degree when they can begin enjoying high pay immediately. The result is a shortage of teachers.

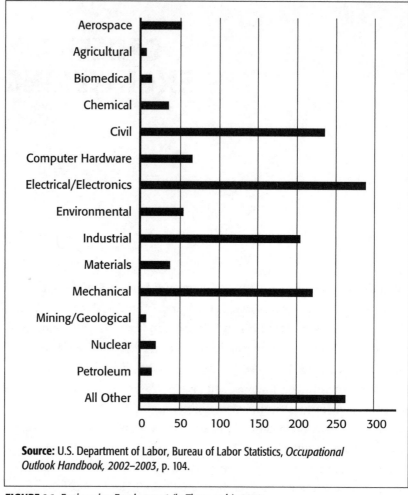

FIGURE 9.1 Engineering Employment (in Thousands), 2000

According to the U. S. Bureau of Labor Statistics, in 2000 there were 1,465,000 engineers (Figure 9.1), of which 179,000 worked for federal, state, and local governments (almost half of these public-sector engineers worked for the federal government, mostly in the Departments of Defense, Energy, Transportation, Agriculture, and Interior and for the National Aeronautics and Space Administration). Some 400,000 engineers worked in services industries, designing buildings and machinery, doing research, testing materials and devices, and providing business services. Over 40,000 engineers were self-employed, mostly as consultants.

Employment of engineers as a group is expected to increase more slowly than the average through 2010. The outlook does vary by specialty, and some specialties are subject to changes in federal expenditures for defense, space, energy, transportation, and environment. Because technology changes steadily and standards are subject to revision, engineers who expect to remain employed must keep their knowledge up-to-date. This means reading journals, attending workshops and conferences, and taking courses throughout their career.

ARCHITECTURE

Architects are both artists and applied physicists as well as materials scientists. They design and supervise the construction of buildings—houses, factories, offices, skyscrapers, airport terminals, hotels, and more. They strive to make their products attractive, usable, energy efficient, sturdy, safe, and economical. They must thus know the strengths, durabilities, and costs of materials; be able to plan how materials will go together and interact; and be able to calculate loads and stresses on each element of a structure. They must also take into account building codes, zoning laws, access laws, and other regulations, and they need skills in drawing and managing. Modern architects must also be familiar with computer-aided design and drafting (CADD).

In 2000, there were 102,000 active architects in this country. All obtained licenses by passing state exams. To qualify to take the exams, they had earned a bachelor's degree in architecture and gained three years of experience working for a licensed architect.

In some cases, experience replaced the bachelor's degree. Most of the nation's 100 accredited architecture programs offer a five-year bachelor's program. There are also master of architecture programs—two years for students with suitable bachelor's training and three to four years for students with other bachelor's degrees.

In 2000, experienced, full-time architects averaged almost $52,510 per year. Architects with a lot of experience and a good reputation made upward of $85,000.

Job openings in architecture seem likely to be in fair supply, with employment rising about as fast as the average for all occupations through the year 2010. However, many young people find architecture an attractive field, so there will be competition, especially for the best jobs. In addition, the job prospects in the field will depend closely on the health of the national economy.

LANDSCAPE ARCHITECTURE

Where architects design and build buildings, *landscape architects* work with space. Given a site, they decide where buildings, roads, parks, and lawns will go. They are planners and artists, and they must have knowledge of wind, sun, rain, drainage, and plant biology. They may also supervise construction and work with architects. Most landscape architects are employed by the landscape and horticultural services industry.

The nation's 22,000 landscape architects enjoy an optimistic job outlook, for their field grows with concern for the environment and for urban and regional planning. Most have a four- or five-year bachelor's degree in landscape architecture; some have a master's degree; in most states, they must be licensed. The median salary for all landscape architects was $43,540 in 2000. Those who worked for the federal government in 2001 averaged $62,824. Employment should increase faster than the average for all occupations through 2010.

SURVEYING, CARTOGRAPHY, AND PHOTOGRAMMETRY

Surveyors are measurers of land. With theodolites, transits, laser instruments, and even satellites and radio telescopes, they measure elevations, distances, contours, angles, and directions. They mark the boundaries of house lots and subdivisions and the routes of new roads, keep tunnels on course and level, and monitor the land surface for bulges that may promise earthquakes and volcanic eruptions. They also record their measurements with maps, sketches, and reports. Their work is essential to *cartography* (mapmaking), construction projects, land valuation, and the preparation of legal deeds. Extreme accuracy is their watchword.

In 2000, there were about 121,000 surveyors, cartographers, photogrammetrists, and surveying technicians in the United States. Some held a bachelor's degree in surveying. Many were graduates of one-, two-, or three-year programs offered by community colleges. The bachelor's degree is most essential for specialized surveyors such as *photogrammetrists*, who work from aerial and satellite photos, but as technology advances, the bachelor's degree is becoming necessary for all surveyors. Other specialists include *land, marine, geodetic,* and *geophysical prospecting surveyors* and *map editors.* The new GPS (Global Positioning System) technology, using satellite signals and handheld receivers, has done much to create geographical information systems (GIS), which match data to location through sophisticated computerized databases. Those who build and work with GIS systems are known as *geographical information specialists.*

All states require that land surveyors be licensed. They must pass at least a national exam prepared by the National Council of Examiners for Engineering and Surveying and often a state exam as well. Many states also require several years of experience.

In 2000, surveyors averaged $36,700 in annual pay. Cartographers and photogrammetrists averaged $39,410. Surveying and mapping technicians averaged about $26,000. In 2001, the federal government paid land surveyors on average $57,416, cartographers $62,369, surveying technicians $34,623, and the more specialized geodetic and cartographic technicians $53,143 and $40,775, respectively.

Employment of surveyors should grow about as fast as the average for all occupations through the year 2010. Those with good technical skills will enjoy the best prospects. Much of the present and future demand is related to construction, urban planning, resource management, and emergency planning.

AEROSPACE ENGINEERING

The American Institute of Aeronautics and Astronautics says that "aerospace engineering and technology is probably the most specialized and yet the most diversified field there is." *Aerospace engineers* design and build aircraft and spacecraft, satellites, rocket engines, guidance systems, nose cones, and more. They deal with the physics of propulsion, fluid mechanics and aerodynamics, thermodynamics, structures, flight and space mechanics, and energy. Outside the aerospace field, they apply their knowledge to energy conservation, to evaluation of the wind loads on a skyscraper, or to the designing of an efficient wind turbine.

Aerospace engineers analyze problems and data, design aerospace devices, do materials and product testing, and work in manufacturing, servicing, marketing, and management. Some work more as scientists than as engineers, doing research and development work for industry or government or teaching and researching on campus.

There were about 50,000 U.S. aerospace engineers in 2000, almost half working in the aerospace industry. Many had no more than a bachelor's degree; master's degrees and doctorates are essential for academic teaching and research and for promotion to senior research and management positions. Employment in the field is expected to grow about as fast as average through 2010.

Aerospace engineers averaged $67,930 in 2000. Those working for the federal government averaged $74,170. In 2001, new bachelor's graduates received average offers of $47,000; new master's graduates were offered almost $60,000; and new doctoral graduates received a bit over $64,000.

AGRICULTURAL ENGINEERING

Agricultural engineers work on the design, construction, testing, selling, and servicing of equipment used for preparing soil and planting, cultivating, harvesting, and processing crops. They also design buildings and equipment for animal care and processing, storage systems, greenhouses, power supplies, control systems, and water supplies. They may work in irrigation, flood control, land reclamation, waste treatment and disposal, soil and water conservation, and land use. They may even work on recreation facilities.

There is and will be good demand for agricultural engineers, and the pay averaged $55,850 in 2000. Most workers in the field need only a bachelor's degree; higher degrees are needed for research and teaching on campus.

BIOMEDICAL ENGINEERING

Biomedical engineers include engineers of all kinds—aerospace, materials, electrical, mechanical—who are interested in medical problems. They design and build medical diagnostic and treatment instruments, imaging systems, prostheses, artificial organs, and more. They develop medical uses for new technologies such as lasers. They adapt computers to the needs of medical data processing and modernize laboratory, hospital, and clinic structures and procedures.

Bioengineers, biotechnologists, or *bioenvironmental engineers* specialize in less medical areas. They work on maintaining and improving environmental quality and protecting plants, animals, and humans from toxic substances and pollutants. *Medical engineers* specialize in medical diagnosis and therapy, developing instruments, materials, devices, computer systems, and artificial organs. *Clinical engineers* concentrate on improving health-care delivery systems.

Most biomedical engineers have a bachelor's degree in an engineering area and a master's or doctorate in biomedical engineering, but bachelor's degrees in biomedical engineering are available. The pay is good, averaging over $57,000 in 2000, and employment is expected to grow faster than average through 2010. Biomedical engineers with advanced degrees will have little trouble finding jobs, especially in teaching and research.

CHEMICAL ENGINEERING

Chemical engineers turn chemistry into products. In research and development, they devise economical and efficient production processes. They then design, construct, and operate equipment and factories that use those processes. Some chemical engineers teach and do research on campus.

There were 33,000 chemical engineers in 2000. Seventy-three percent of all chemical engineers worked in manufacturing industries, dealing with electronics, pharmaceuticals, cosmetics, paints, dyes, pesticides, fertilizers, and petroleum refining. Chemical engineers also work on the purification of polluted water and air; pollution prevention; waste management; the recycling of metals, glass, and plastics; and the development of solar and geothermal energy. In every case, they need problem-solving and computer skills.

The usual preparation for a career in chemical engineering involves a four- or five-year bachelor of science in the field. Higher degrees are essential for careers on campus and helpful for senior research and management positions in industry and government. Average pay in the field was $65,960 in 2000. A bachelor-level chemical engineer could start at about $51,000 in 2001; a master's graduate, at $57,000; and a doctorate, at over $75,000. Chemical engineers typically earn several thousand dollars more a year than chemists.

Despite the dependence of industry on chemical engineers, job openings in the field are expected to grow more slowly than the average for all occupations through the year 2010. Much of the growth will be in the plastics, materials, biotechnology, pharmaceuticals, and electronics industries.

CIVIL ENGINEERING

Often working closely with other engineers and architects, *civil engineers* design and oversee the construction of buildings, roads and highways, railways, airports, tunnels, bridges, and water supply and sewage systems. Their specialties include soil mechanics and structural, hydraulic, environmental or sanitary, transportation, and highway engineering. Over half the nation's 232,000 civil engineers work for engineering consulting firms. A third work for federal, state, and local governments. Most of the rest are employed by the construction industry.

A bachelor's degree is essential for a career in civil engineering, but a master's degree is becoming more and more necessary for continued, effective functioning. The employment outlook is quite favorable, for the U.S. population is still growing (albeit slowly), and the next few years will call for a fair amount of design and construction of new manufacturing plants, water supply and transportation systems, and pollution control facilities.

Pay averaged $55,740 in 2000, with the federal government paying about 12 percent more than that. In 2001, bachelor's graduates could start at over $40,000, master's graduates at $44,000, and doctoral graduates at over $62,000.

COMPUTER HARDWARE ENGINEERING

Computer hardware engineers develop and test computer chips, circuit boards, systems, and components. Because computers have become integral to the functioning of every modern business (including colleges and universities and government offices) and home, and because they are now found in automobiles, home appliances, and a great many other devices, this field of engineering is essential to the operation of modern society.

There were about 60,000 computer hardware engineers in 2000. Median pay was $67,300; in the computer and office equipment industry, it topped $75,000. In 2001, bachelor's graduates received average starting offers of $53,924; master's graduates could start at $58,000; and doctoral graduates, at over $70,000.

ELECTRICAL AND ELECTRONICS ENGINEERING

Electrical and electronics engineering is a diverse field. Among the many technical societies that belong to the Institute of Electrical and Electronics Engineers (IEEE) are ones for specialists in robotics, lasers, nanotechnology, signal processing, aerospace systems, antennas, radio and television, communications, manufacturing technology, computers, management, biomedicine, nuclear power, social implications of technology, cybernetics, vehicular technology, and more. In other words, *electrical and electronics engineers* find work wherever electrical and electronic equipment is used and wherever electrical and electronic phenomena arise. They develop new products, test and maintain equipment, solve operating problems, and manage projects. Many are involved in selling.

Most of the nation's 288,000 electrical and electronics engineers have a bachelor's degree. Higher degrees are in greatest demand on campus and in senior management. Employment should grow about as fast as the average for all occupations through 2010. Many of the best jobs are in the computer industry, and employers there compete fiercely for the best workers.

Median pay was nearly $65,000 in 2000. In 2001, bachelor's graduates could start at almost $52,000, master's graduates at $64,000, and doctoral graduates at over $79,000.

ENVIRONMENTAL ENGINEERING

Environmental engineers apply chemistry and biology to water and air pollution control, recycling, waste (including hazardous waste) disposal, and public health. Their focus may be local, as when they design a sewage treatment plant, or global, as when they analyze and attempt to cope with global warming.

There were about 52,000 environmental engineers in 2000, almost a third of them working for federal, state, or local government. Employment is expected to increase faster than average through 2010, although the prospects are subject to political trends. Median earnings were almost $58,000 in 2000. In 2001, bachelor's graduates could start at over $51,000.

INDUSTRIAL ENGINEERING

In 2000, this nation employed about 198,000 industrial (including health and safety) engineers, mostly in the manufacturing industries, but also in insurance companies, banks, construction and mining firms, utilities, and hospitals. Some industrial engineers work in government as regulators and inspectors, and some work on campus.

Industrial engineers focus on how best to coordinate people, machines, and materials. They design production lines, do long-range planning, and work on computerized information systems, among other things. Many wind up in management, and advancement is typically rapid.

The related *manufacturing engineers* concentrate on manufacturing processes. They devise new methods and specify the details of standard methods for new products. They also design and set up manufacturing equipment, and they are essential to efficient production. *Health and safety engineers* focus on work site and product safety.

Only a bachelor's degree in the field is necessary for most jobs. Higher degrees aid, but are not essential to, promotion; they are necessary only on campus. Employment should grow more slowly than the average for all occupations through the year 2010.

Median pay for industrial engineers was $58,850 in 2000. Health and safety engineers averaged $54,630. In 2001, bachelor's graduates could start at over $48,000, master's graduates at $56,000, and doctoral graduates at about $60,000.

MATERIALS ENGINEERING

Materials engineers deal with producing, processing, and testing the metals, ceramics, polymers, and other materials necessary to manufacture the many products we use. *Metallurgical engineers* deal with ores, the extraction of metals from them, and the refining, alloying, casting, fabricating, and heat treating of the metals. In research, they strive to develop better methods of doing all these things, sometimes even coming up with biological techniques, such as the use of acid-secreting bacteria to leach metal compounds from copper and uranium ores. Metallurgical engineers also design, develop, and operate plants and equipment for their field.

Metallurgical engineers may specialize in *physical metallurgy*, the study and analysis of the properties of metals; in *mechanical* or *extractive* or *chemical metallurgy*, the separation of metals from ores; in *process engineering*, plant design and processing techniques; and in *materials science*, the study of the properties and uses of metals and nonmetallic materials (including ceramics and plastics). Metallurgical engineers are crucial to transportation, communications, and energy systems. And because metal processing—especially the smelting of metals from ores—contributes so much to industrial pollution, these engineers are often deeply involved with society's concern for the environment.

Ceramic engineers work with nonmetallic, inorganic materials—ceramics. They match ceramics to intended uses, develop new ceramics, and devise the machinery for making and shaping them.

Eighty-four percent of the nation's 33,000 metallurgical, ceramic, and materials engineers work in manufacturing. Some work for government and on campus. Employment is expected to be strongest in the electronics and plastics industries but to decline in metals and ceramics. Overall, employment will grow more slowly than average through 2010. A bachelor's degree is enough to enter the field. Metallurgical engineers with higher degrees find employment in research and on campus.

Materials engineers averaged $59,000 in 2000. In 2001, bachelor's graduates could expect starting offers of almost $50,000.

MECHANICAL ENGINEERING

Some *mechanical engineers* are industrial, biomedical, automotive, agricultural, or aerospace engineers. They are concerned with mechanical devices of various kinds, from can openers to automobile transmissions and engines to rocket fuel pumps. They work in the conversion of energy from natural sources—the sun, wind, water, heat, coal, oil, atoms—to useful forms. They design and develop machines that provide and use power. Many work in the transportation, electric utility, heating, and cooling industries.

Mechanical engineers may specialize in the needs of a particular industry, such as the paper, textile, construction, petroleum, or automobile industry; in marine equipment; in energy conversion systems; in materials handling; in production equipment; in heating, ventilating, and air-conditioning systems; or in instrumentation.

Many mechanical engineers work in the design and development of new devices, and here they find computer-aided design/computer-aided manufacturing (CAD/CAM) software indispensable. Others work in maintenance, production, sales, and management. Some teach on campus. All are professional problem solvers: given a need, they can either design a solution or point to the necessary device.

There were 221,000 mechanical engineers in the United States in 2000. Over half of them worked in the manufacturing industries. Most had a four- or five-year bachelor's degree in the field. Some had a higher degree. The job outlook is adequate for the next few years, partly because of the growing complexity of industrial processes. The pay runs a little worse than that for electrical engineers, with the median pay in 2000 running at near $59,000. In 2001, bachelor's graduates could start at over $48,000, master's graduates at $56,000, and doctoral graduates at about $72,000.

MINING AND GEOLOGICAL ENGINEERING

Mining and geological engineers (including *mining safety engineers*) combine the fields of geology and metallurgical engineering. One specialty, in fact, is that of the *mining geologist*, who seeks new sources of minerals. *Mining engineers* are in charge of extracting the minerals once they are discovered by the mining geologist. They design and supervise the construction of open-pit and underground mines, oversee the construction of ore transportation systems and living facilities for the miners, and are responsible for safe ventilation, abundant power and water supplies, communications, and maintenance. *Mineral processing engineers* direct the separation of minerals from their ore by crushing, grinding, and chemical treatment. *Mining safety engineers* design the mines, equipment, and procedures that ensure the safety of all the mine workers and comply with a myriad of government health and safety regulations.

Mining engineers often specialize in a particular mineral. Thus, there are such specialties as *coal mining engineers, copper mining engineers*, and *uranium mining engineers*. In each case, the engineer faces special problems of extraction, safety, and environmental protection. The last often includes restoring a worked-out mine to a condition approximating that of the land before the mine was opened.

In 2000, there were about 6,500 mining engineers in this country, each with a bachelor's degree in his or her field. Those with higher degrees find work in research and on campus. Most mining engineers work for mining companies or manufacturers of mining equipment. The job outlook is poor, for employment is expected to decline through the year 2010. The reason is that domestic demand for coal, metal, and other minerals is not expected to grow very much. However, foreign demand for graduates of U.S. mining engineering programs is high; those willing to work abroad should not lack for employment.

Mining and geological engineers (including mining safety engineers) averaged in 2000 about $61,000 per year. In 2001, new bachelor's graduates received average starting offers of $42,500. New master's graduates were offered $54,000.

NUCLEAR ENGINEERING

Nuclear engineers are mechanical engineers who specialize in the design, construction, and operation of nuclear power plants on land and at sea. They may also do research, work on nuclear fuels, design and build nuclear weapons, and find industrial and medical uses for radioactive materials. Safety is often their main concern. In nuclear power plants, they must be able to respond immediately and correctly to any of a wide range of problems. When they fail, the consequences may include exposure of thousands of people to life-threatening radiation, as happened in the Chernobyl disaster in the Ukraine.

There were about 14,000 nuclear engineers in the United States in 2000. Fifty-five percent worked for utility companies, and 14 percent worked for the federal government. About a quarter worked in engineering consulting firms. In 2000, pay averaged just over $79,000. In 2001, new bachelor's graduates received average starting offers of $49,600; new master's graduates were offered $56,300.

Employment is not expected to change through the year 2010, largely because of safety concerns about nuclear power, but decision makers are beginning to realize that nuclear power may actually be safer in the long run than fossil fuels, which threaten to warm climate, raise sea level, and even spread tropical diseases into Northern Hemisphere nations. Currently, most job openings are expected to result from the need to replace current employees as they retire or take up other jobs, but that could change if we get serious about preventing global warming.

PETROLEUM ENGINEERING

Petroleum engineers are essentially mining engineers who deal with oil and gas. They explore and drill for these fossil fuels, striving to maximize their recovery by such tactics as injecting steam, detergents, and water into wells to force out the oil and gas. At present, oil companies can recover only about half of the oil or gas in a deposit tapped by a well. With shortages looming—oil supply is expected to peak in the next few years—and fuel prices high, petroleum engineers thus spend much of their time trying to increase recovery rates. In addition, they do research on and supervise well drilling on land and at sea.

There were about 9,000 petroleum engineers in 2000. Most worked in the petroleum industry. Some worked for federal and state governments and on campus. Most had a bachelor's degree. Those with higher degrees worked in research and on campus.

The job outlook is poor, with employment expected to decline through the year 2010 unless the prices of oil and gas rise significantly. In time, many new jobs will involve new sources of oil, such as oil shale, and the application of petroleum engineering techniques to other areas, such as drilling wells to tap geothermal energy.

Petroleum engineers earned a median pay in 2000 of $78,910. In 2001, new bachelor's graduates received average starting offers of $54,000; new master's graduates were offered $58,500.

ENGINEERING TECHNICIANS AND TECHNOLOGISTS

Like the life, earth, physical, and space sciences, engineering provides jobs for numerous technicians. In 2000, in fact, all fields of engineering together employed some 519,000 technicians, 35 percent of them in manufacturing. About 230,000 were electrical and electronics engineering technicians. The jobs of engineering technicians are more limited in scope than those of engineers or scientists, and they require less training and carry less pay. The training frequently consists of a two-year community college or technical institute program. Training can also come on the job or in the military.

The engineering technician's work may lie in any area of technology—aeronautical engineering; air-conditioning, heating, and refrigeration; civil engineering; biomedical engineering; electronics; chemical engineering; manufacturing; industrial engineering; mechanical engineering; instrumentation; and more. The work generally consists of operating equipment and instruments, making measurements, doing calculations, and otherwise following the instructions of a supervising engineer. Engineering technicians may also work in sales, technical writing, or maintenance or as service representatives.

In 2000, electrical and electronics engineering technicians averaged about $40,000; civil engineering technicians averaged $36,000; aerospace engineering and operations technicians averaged $53,000; environmental engineering technicians averaged $30,000; mechanical engineering technicians could expect a little over $40,000. Pay did depend on the industry in which one worked: industrial engineering technicians could expect over $73,000 in computer and data processing services but only $36,000 in electrical components and accessories. The job prospects are excellent across the board.

The Labor Department counts separately 213,000 drafters, who prepare engineering and architectural drawings and blueprints. Their pay is comparable to that of technicians, and the necessary education is the same; employers actually prefer drafters who have technical training. The job prospects are best for those with a two-year degree in drafting and with training or experience with computer-aided drafting systems.

The National Institute for Certification in Engineering Technologies (NICET; nicet.org) also recognizes the engineering technologist occupation:

NICET defines *engineering technicians* as the "hands-on" members of the engineering team who work under the direction of engineers, scientists, and technologists. They have knowledge of the components, operating characteristics, and limitations of engineering systems and processes particular to their area of specialization.

The Institute defines *engineering technologists* as members of the engineering team who work closely with engineers, scientists, and technicians. Technologists have a thorough knowledge of the equipment, applications, and established state-of-the-art design and implementation methods in a particular engineering area.

Where the engineer designs, plans, constructs, operates, and maintains complete technical devices and systems, the technologist solves technical problems, organizing people, materials, and equipment to design, operate, maintain, and manage technical engineering projects. It seems clear that the engineering technologist must do many of the same things as engineers, albeit with a somewhat more operational emphasis. As a field, engineering technology is too new to appear in the Labor Department's *Occupational Outlook Handbook*. It exists, for it is mentioned in the career brochures of many engineering societies and students can earn four-year bachelor's degrees in it, but it is apparently still splitting away from engineering as the latter has been defined. Many people become technologists by transferring into a four-year program after completing a two-year degree as an engineering technician.

HOT SPOTS

The most exciting careers for the immediate future still lie in the booming technology of information handling—computers and communications. Biomedical engineering is already flourishing and should do even better in coming years. Chemical engineers will remain in demand, as will petroleum and mining engineers. Materials science, especially in the new field of nanotechnology, will provide fascinating work. A good indication of where things are going can be found in *Technology Review's* annual list of "10 Emerging Technologies That Will Change the World." The 2003 list included the engineering-related items of wireless sensor networks, tissue engineering, nano solar cells, mechatronics (mechanical devices integrated with computer hardware and software), molecular imaging, and nanoimprint lithography.

According to the Bureau of Labor Statistics of the U.S. Department of Labor, engineering as a single field can expect to see a 9 percent (138,000 jobs) growth in employment from 2000 to 2010. The three subfields of engineering that can expect the greatest percentage growth are biomedical engineering (31%), computer hardware engineering (25%), and environmental engineering (26%). In addition, landscape architects can expect 31 percent growth. Numerically, the lead settles on civil engineers (24,000 jobs), electrical and electronics engineers (31,000), and mechanical engineers (29,000).

CAREERS ON CAMPUS

Of the nation's 1,465,000 (BLS estimate) engineers of all kinds, about 5 percent work on campus, and there is constant concern that not enough young engineers are pursuing doctorates in their fields with an eye toward academic careers. Industrial pay scales are too tempting. Relatively few students are willing to stay in school, struggling to win a degree that will qualify them for research and teaching at less pay than they can earn in industry with just a bachelor's degree. The average salary for full-time faculty was $58,000 in 2000, with first-time faculty (assistant professors) averaging only $45,600. With only a bachelor's degree, engineers in some fields could start at considerably higher pay. With a doctorate, *starting* pay ranged from $60,000 to $80,000. With experience, engineering faculty can expect over $90,000, even without higher degrees.

However, some young engineers do choose an academic career. They prefer the work environment on campus, or they are dedicated to teaching. They also enjoy the opportunity to supplement their income with a variety of consulting jobs. Nevertheless, the nation's colleges and universities are concerned that too few are entering academic careers to ensure an adequate supply of trained engineers for the future. Some schools are thus raising the pay for their engineering faculty, even seeking funds from state and federal governments and from industry to become more competitive with industry.

We should note that a number of museums of science and technology employ engineers in the preparation of exhibits and in related research. Campus-affiliated research centers, such as the Jet Propulsion Laboratory in Pasadena, California, also employ engineers.

CAREERS IN INDUSTRY

Most engineers—about 80 percent of the total—work in industry and enjoy high pay. Some do applied research. Most are involved in manufacturing, construction, production, and planning. Many work in management, sales, maintenance, technical writing, and other areas.

CAREERS IN GOVERNMENT

About 14 percent of all engineers are employed by federal, state, or local government. They work in federal planning and construction programs, state highway departments, and municipal public service departments. The federal government uses engineers in the military, perhaps especially in the Army Corps of Engineers, and elsewhere in the Defense Department. The Departments of Energy, Agriculture, Transportation, and Interior also employ engineers, as does NASA. Some federal engineers are industrial safety inspectors; energy regulators; congressional staffers, advisers, and fellows; and even astronauts.

ORGANIZATIONS FOR ENGINEERS

There are a few all-inclusive engineering societies, such as the Accreditation Board for Engineering and Technology, the National Society of Professional Engineers, and the American Society for Engineering Education. They offer a variety of career-related publications and lists of schools with approved engineering programs. See the list for their addresses and websites.

In addition, every engineering specialty has its own professional society. Most of these societies provide career information on their websites. Some supply help to young engineers seeking jobs. All hold periodic meetings at which the members deliver papers, socialize, and make contacts that may lead to future job offers. Employers also attend these meetings, often with the aim of recruiting employees.

It is worth noting that very few engineers belong to minority groups. In 1972, only 1,300 of 43,000 engineering graduates were black, Hispanic, or Native American. Since then, the National Action Council for Minorities in Engineering (NACME) has used corporate and foundation funds to provide scholarships for minority engineering students. By 1999, blacks alone accounted for 37,700 working engineers, and all minority groups together accounted for 18 percent of all engineers.

Societies and Sources of Further Information for Careers In Engineering

Accreditation Board for Engineering and Technology
111 Market Place, Suite 1050
Baltimore, MD 21202-4012
www.abet.org

American Academy of Environmental Engineers
130 Holiday Court, Suite 100
Annapolis, MD 21401
www.enviro-engrs.org

American Association for Geodetic Surveying
6 Montgomery Village Avenue, Suite 403
Gaithersburg, MD 20879
www.acsm.net/aags/index.html

American Chemical Society
1155 16th Street, NW
Washington, DC 20036
www.chemistry.org/portal/chemistry

American Congress on Surveying and Mapping
6 Montgomery Village Avenue, Suite 403
Gaithersburg, MD 20879
www.acsm.net/index.html

American Indian Science and Engineering Society (AISES)
P.O. Box 9828
Albuquerque, NM 87119-9828
www.aises.org

American Institute of Aeronautics and Astronautics
1801 Alexander Bell Drive, Suite 500
Reston, VA 20191-4344
www.aiaa.org

American Institute of Architects
1735 New York Avenue, NW
Washington, DC 20006
www.aia.org

American Institute of Chemical Engineers
3 Park Avenue
New York, NY 10016-5991
www.aiche.org

American Nuclear Society
555 N. Kensington Avenue
La Grange Park, IL 60526
www.ans.org

American Society for Engineering Education
1818 N Street, NW, Suite 600
Washington, DC 20036-2479
www.asee.org

American Society for Photogrammetry and Remote Sensing
5410 Grosvenor Lane, Suite 210
Bethesda, MD 20814-2160
www.asprs.org

American Society of Agricultural Engineers
2950 Niles Road
St. Joseph, MO 49085
www.asae.org

American Society of Civil Engineers
1801 Alexander Bell Drive
Reston, VA 20191-4400
www.asce.org

American Society of Landscape Architects
636 Eye Street, NW
Washington, DC 20001
www.asla.org

American Society of Mechanical Engineers
Three Park Avenue
New York, NY 10016-5990
www.asme.org

American Society of Mining, Metallurgical, and Petroleum Engineers
Three Park Avenue
New York, NY 10016-5998
www.aimeny.org

Biomedical Engineering Society
8401 Corporate Drive, Suite 225
Landover, MD 20785-2224
www.bmes.org

Institute of Electrical and Electronics Engineers, Inc.
1828 L Street, NW, Suite 1202
Washington, DC 20036-5104
www.ieee.org/portal/index.jsp

Institute of Industrial Engineers
3577 Parkway Lane, Suite 200
Norcross, GA 30092
www.iienet.org

Junior Engineering Technical Society
1420 King Street, Suite 405
Alexandria, VA 22314-2794
www.jets.org

Minerals, Metals, and Materials Society
184 Thorn Hill Road
Warrendale, PA 15086-7514
www.tms.org/tmshome.html

National Action Council for Minorities in Engineering (NACME)
350 Fifth Avenue, Suite 2212
New York NY 10118-2299
www.nacme.org

National Organization for the Professional Advancement of
    Black Chemists and Chemical Engineers
P.O. Box 77040
Washington, DC 20013
www.nobcche.org

National Society of Professional Engineers
1420 King Street
Alexandria, VA 22314-2794
www.nspe.org

National Society of Professional Surveyors
6 Montgomery Village Avenue, Suite 403
Gaithersburg, MD 20879
www.acsm.net/nsps/index.html

SM International (Metallurgy)
9639 Kinsman Road
Materials Park, OH 44073-0002
www.asm-intl.org

Society for Mining, Metallurgy, and Exploration
8307 Shaffer Parkway
P.O. Box 277002
Littleton, CO 80127
www.smenet.org

Society of Automotive Engineers
400 Commonwealth Drive
Warrendale, PA 15096-0001
www.sae.org/servlets/index

Society of Manufacturing Engineers
P.O. Box 930
One SME Drive
Dearborn, MI 48121
www.sme.org

Society of Petroleum Engineers
P.O. Box 833836
Richardson, TX 75083-3836
www.spe.org

10

CAREERS IN MATHEMATICS AND COMPUTER SCIENCES

Mathematics is in some ways a peculiar field. For all its dedication to preciseness and system, for all its equations and graphs, it is not quite a science. It cannot be, for it cannot use the scientific method, at least not in the usual sense. A mathematician cannot make observations or perform experiments. Modern mathematicians do, however, find that where equations and theorems cannot deal with a problem, computers can be used to test all imaginable special cases. This is how it was finally proved that four colors are enough to color any map (www.math.utah.edu/~alfeld/math/4color.html).

What, then, is mathematics? It is the study and exploitation of the intrinsic properties of numbers. It is also the invention and exploration of rules of relationship and the manipulation of symbols (which may or may not refer to numbers). It is thus close kin to computer science, and most early computer workers had a background in mathematics. Mathematics approaches science most closely as a tool of science when it deals with actual phenomena in measurement, calculation, and statistics. Otherwise, it is far more an art, its product flowing according to definite and often elaborate rules from the mind of the mathematician.

The distinction between mathematics as science and mathematics as art is neither arbitrary nor artificial. "Pure," or theoretical, mathematicians, like basic researchers in other fields, guide their work solely according to the dictates of curiosity. In fact, they often pride themselves on the irrelevance of their work to the real world. They build abstract algebras—systems of rules and relations—and explore the properties of numbers, interconnected lines ("graphs" and "knots"), and algebraic equations. Happily, their work often finds applications in physics, chemistry, cartography, and cryptography, among others. In fact, work on the factoring of large—100 to 200 digits—numbers led directly to modern near-unbreakable secret codes. Oddly, some pure mathematicians seem to feel offended when their beautifully useless constructions turn out to be useful after all.

"Applied" mathematicians are more interested in the uses of math. They use their knowledge of differential equations, calculus, algebra, probability, and so on, to solve problems in economics, biology, engineering, physics, and other fields. They observe a scientific or technical problem, hypothesize a mathematical approach to the problem, and experiment to see whether the approach works. They thus use a form of the scientific method, and they are much more scientists in the sense we are most familiar with. Pure mathematicians are like artists in their motivations and in the way their work flows from within themselves rather than from without.

Like other scientists, applied mathematicians have to live with the unattainability of ultimate truth. Only their observations—the problems they face and the data they work with—are facts. Their solutions may work, but they may also be open to improvement. Pure mathematicians, on the other hand, do know truth. If they make no errors, then the logical edifices they construct from a handful of rules are immune to argument or improvement. They can only be extended.

Upper-level careers in research and teaching are available in pure and applied mathematics. At lower levels, mathematicians are accountants, actuaries, bookkeepers, and statisticians. When they become more interested in the machinery of computation than in the process or results, they enter the computer sciences as designers, operators, programmers, and service technicians.

MATHEMATICS

Some 20,000 *mathematicians* (including academic statisticians) were employed on campus in the year 2000, teaching and doing pure and applied research. Another 3,600 held jobs as nonacademic mathematicians, working in the communications, chemical, aerospace, computer, and data processing industries and for the federal government, especially in the Department of Defense.

Almost all *pure,* or *theoretical, mathematicians* are employed by colleges and universities, largely because their research is not immediately useful to industry and government. They must generally have a doctorate in their field, and they earn pay comparable to that of other faculty members.

Applied mathematicians find jobs in a greater variety of places, and they can go to work after obtaining a bachelor's, master's, or doctoral degree. New bachelor's graduates started in 2001 at an average salary of $46,466. New master's graduates averaged $55,938. Median annual pay for all mathematicians approached $70,000. In the federal government, mathematicians and mathematical statisticians averaged over $76,000 in 2001. *Cryptanalysts,* who work with commercial and national security encryption systems, made $71,000.

The work of the applied mathematician can involve constructing models to forecast sales; allocating services and resources in a firm or a political unit; calculating the strength, safety, and cost of designs for buildings and machines; studying chemical reactions; and simulating complex devices, such as nuclear reactors and spacecraft. The actual process of work involves several steps:

1. Defining a problem or question
2. Breaking the problem into components and verbally describing their relationships
3. Refining the descriptions of components and relationships in mathematical terms, using equations, inequalities, variables, and other devices (this amounts to constructing a mathematical model, either on paper or as a computer model or simulation)
4. Pulling together the data necessary to plug numbers into the model's equations and checking to see that the model accurately reflects the original problem
5. Solving the model's equations
6. Evaluating and interpreting the results to make the limits of their applicability clear and to explain how to use the results

Mathematicians with a bachelor's degree may solve many problems themselves. Perhaps more often, they are involved in managing large data collections; computing statistics; designing, operating, and programming computers; and teaching high school. They may become actuaries (discussed shortly).

Mathematicians with a master's degree may teach in community colleges and some four-year schools. In industry and government, they may be part of research and problem-solving teams in engineering, physics, chemistry, and forecasting.

Mathematicians holding a doctorate can teach at colleges and universities, do original research, and lead research and problem-solving teams. They may also become independent consultants.

Because most mathematicians work on campus, the job outlook is not as bright as it is in some other fields. The U.S. Department of Labor expects employment to decline through the year 2010. The best opportunities will be for those with doctorates. More jobs will exist in industry and government than on campus, especially in areas related to engineering and computers. The best use of a bachelor's degree in mathematics may be as preparation for graduate work in another science.

STATISTICS

Statisticians are specialists in probability. They analyze data and report on the odds that an average, say, is a true measurement of some quantity and not a chance peculiarity of the data collection process. They develop new tests for the significance of data and apply old tests. They apply their knowledge to the design of psychological and achievement tests; the calculation of insurance premiums; the analysis and design of breeding experiments in agriculture and laboratory genetics; the calculation of the odds that a child will have a birth defect; market analysis and forecasting; weather forecasting; economics; drug, pesticide, and pollutant evaluation; quality control; social science survey design and interpretation; political polling; and more.

The 19,000 U.S. statisticians in 2000 worked largely in private industry. Over half worked in the manufacturing, insurance, public relations, testing, and computer industries. A fifth worked for the federal government, especially for the Departments of Commerce, Labor, Health and Human Services, and Agriculture. The rest worked on campus, teaching and doing research.

Many jobs are available to bachelor's graduates, but the demand is strongest and the pay is best for statisticians with master's and doctor's degrees. In 2000, statisticians enjoyed a median pay of $51,990. In 2001, federal government statisticians averaged $68,900 per year.

For statisticians, employment is not expected to change much through 2010. Those with training in other fields, such as engineering or sociology, will fare best. Many jobs will be available in quality control, business forecasting, economics, management, the evaluation of drugs and other substances, and government programs. Much of the demand for statisticians is due to the ever-growing insistence on reducing risks of all kinds in safety-related fields, in health, and in business. This demand is not likely to change unless the costs of error fall drastically.

ACCOUNTING

The nation's 976,000 *accountants* and *auditors* are concerned with financial records. They keep track of expenditures, income, profit, and loss; prepare financial reports; and calculate taxes. Auditors tend to emphasize checking the financial records and reports of companies and individuals for conformity to truth and law.

Public accountants work for themselves or for accounting firms and prepare and audit financial records. *Management* (or *industrial* or *private*) accountants work for a company and handle its financial records. *Government accountants* and *auditors* deal with the records of government agencies and audit private companies and individuals; many work for the Internal Revenue Service.

Accountants may specialize in auditing, taxes, management consulting, or computer systems. Some serve business and professional schools as teachers, researchers, and administrators. A great many find the field congenial because there are many opportunities for part-time work, especially in small firms and in the preparation of tax returns.

Most accounting jobs require a bachelor's degree in accounting. Many employers ask for a master's degree in accounting or a master's of business administration (M.B.A.) with an accounting concentration. Most accountants find highly valuable the certificates in public accounting (C.P.A.), management accounting, and internal auditing awarded upon examination by state boards of accountancy and the professional societies.

The job outlook is excellent, especially for accountants with computer experience, professional certification, and/or a master's degree. In 2000, the median pay for accountants and auditors was $43,500. Those working in computer and data processing services averaged $47,000. The pay started in 2001 at about $30,000 for beginning accountants and auditors. Experienced auditors could earn $35,000 to $60,000. Experienced senior accountants earned $75,000 and up. In 2001, the federal government started junior accountants and auditors at $21,947. A superior academic record raised that to $27,185. A master's degree or two years of experience brought $33,254. In 2001, federal accountants averaged $64,770; auditors averaged $67,180.

ACTUARIAL SCIENCE

Actuaries are statisticians who work for insurance companies and financial institutions. They calculate the probabilities of death, illness, disability, unemployment, retirement, and property loss. They use their calculations to compute expected payouts for insurance companies and pension funds and to set premiums that will allow their employers to make a profit. They may specialize in life, health, property, or liability insurance or in pension plans. As executives, they help set company policy. Actuaries who work for state and federal governments may work with government insurance and pension plans or serve as regulators of the private insurance and pension industries.

There were about 14,000 actuaries in 2000, most employed in the insurance industry. Only a few taught on campus. Almost all had a bachelor's degree in mathematics, statistics, actuarial science, economics, finance, or accounting. Higher degrees were relatively scarce. Advancement depends on passing a series of examinations given by the Society of Actuaries and the Casualty Actuarial Society. Preparation for the exams takes extensive home study, and the whole series of exams takes five to ten years. Those who pass the whole series in their specialty become full members of their societies and earn the title of "fellow."

Job growth for actuaries will be less than the average for all occupations through the year 2010. The best opportunities will be for college graduates who have passed at least two of the actuarial exams while still in school. The best prospects should be in the computer and data processing, health services, and management and actuarial consulting industries.

In 2000, the median pay for actuaries was $66,590. In 2001, federal actuaries averaged $78,120. New bachelor's graduates averaged about $46,000 in 2001. Experienced actuaries who passed about half of their professional exams and earned the rank of "associate" could expect over $90,000 per year. Fellows averaged almost $110,000.

BOOKKEEPING

Bookkeeping, accounting, and *auditing clerks* keep the financial records of businesses, prepare financial statements and bills, write checks, and calculate payrolls. In small businesses, they may have full responsibility for financial matters. In larger firms, they may work under a head bookkeeper or accountant.

Most of the nation's 1,991,000 bookkeeping, accounting, and auditing clerk jobs require no more than a high school diploma with courses in bookkeeping, business math, and accounting principles. The best opportunities go to graduates of bookkeeping programs at community colleges and business schools. Skill with computers and accounting software helps greatly.

The U.S. Department of Labor expects bookkeeping employment to remain stable through the year 2010. However, employee turnover is high, so no bookkeeper need stay unemployed for long. In 2000, the pay averaged about $24,000 ($12.34 per hour).

COMPUTER SCIENCE

In the past few years, the computer information technology (IT) industry and related businesses have suffered badly. Many companies (the infamous "dot-coms") have failed. Computer "techies" can no longer expect the high salaries of the 1990s. Yet the computer industry continues to employ a great many people, and it will need many more in future years as businesses rely more and more on computers for collecting, storing, interchanging, and analyzing data. At the same time, a great many IT workers are nearing retirement and will need to be replaced; the National Academy of Public Administration (NAPA) reported in 2003 that of 60,000 federal IT workers, half will need to be replaced by 2010. The skills most in demand are expected to involve computer security, project management, and large-scale systems design.

At the highest levels, the field employs *information* and *computer scientists* in the design of new computers, computer languages, and related devices and in research into new ways to use computers effectively. These people often belong to the Institute of Electrical and Electronics Engineers (IEEE; see Chapter 9) or the Association for Computing Machinery (ACM). Some of their most exciting work is in the fields of robotics and artificial intelligence, where they strive to design machines that can imitate or duplicate various aspects of human intelligence, from pattern recognition to problem solving (in chess, geometry, algebra, and other areas).

COMPUTER OPERATIONS

At somewhat lower levels are the people who operate, program, and service computers. *Computer operators* enter data and instructions at typewriter keyboards and operate and control the computer, attaching peripheral equipment as necessary and watching for error signals. They maintain files of data and programs on computer-readable media. Many people in this field work with networked personal computers and as managers of computer services such as America OnLine, EarthLink, and local Internet service providers.

In 2000, there were about 194,000 computer operators. (Data entry and information processing clerks numbered an additional 806,000.) Because of increased automation, employment in this field should decline sharply through the year 2010. The best opportunities will go to those who gain some post–high school training in computer operations in a community college, business school, or computer or vocational school. Training is also available in the military and on the job. Experience is essential for the best jobs.

Most jobs that require relatively little education do not pay exceedingly well. In 2000, computer operators averaged $27,670. In 2001, the federal government paid computer operators an average of $37,574 a year. Better pay comes with further education and a change in job, perhaps to computer programmer.

COMPUTER PROGRAMMING

The 2000 roster of *computer programmers* included some 585,000 persons. Programmers are responsible for telling computers what to do with the data they are fed by their operators. Programmers write step-by-step instructions in one of many "computer languages." They must be able to think excruciatingly logically and to break down any process into its smallest steps.

Programmers work with mailing lists, payrolls, databases, mathematical computations, and models of complex mechanical, economic, and weather systems. They invent video games, and they write the software packages that allow personal computers to balance budgets, compute statistics and taxes, and act as word processors. In every case, they must remove all errors from, or "debug," their programs so they will work. Their work ends with the preparation of instructions or documentation for the computer operator or the end user of the software.

Most computer programmers have a bachelor's degree. Often the degree is in a field such as accounting, engineering, or mathematics, with additional courses in computer programming (offered today in almost every two-year and four-year school). Many more have a bachelor's degree in information or computer science. Some jobs, especially on campus and in industrial or government research and development, require a master's degree or doctorate. Almost no jobs exist for programmers without some college education. Continuing education is essential for any programmer who wishes to keep up with the rapid changes in computer technology. However, workers in the field may be less concerned with adding degrees to their résumé than with expanding their "skill set" with training programs and courses offered by employers, software vendors, and academic institutions.

There are many opportunities for advancement for skilled workers. In large organizations, programmers can move up to supervisory and management positions. Any programmer can cut loose to become a self-employed consultant or software specialist, often as part of the industry that has arisen to supply packaged programs for personal computers. The job prospects are good, with the field expected to grow about as fast as average through the year 2010. The best opportunities will be for men and women with bachelor's or higher degrees.

In 2000, full-time programmers averaged about $57,500 per year. Highly skilled programmers could earn over $90,000. In 2001, new bachelor's graduates received average starting offers of $48,600. Applications development programmers/developers could start at $60,000 to $90,000. Software development programmers/analysts could start at $54,000 to $78,000. Internet programmers/analysts could start at $56,000 to $84,000.

COMPUTER SOFTWARE ENGINEERING

Computer software engineers begin with user needs to design, develop, test, and evaluate computer programs and IT systems. They need advanced programming skills but are more concerned with devising techniques (algorithms) and planning programs for others to code. They may specialize in applications software, systems software, or networks. They often work in teams with hardware engineers, systems analysts, and others.

In 2000, there were about 697,000 computer software engineers in the United States. Almost half worked in the computer and data processing services industry, which develops and sells prepackaged and custom software, designs systems, and provides Internet services.

Computer software engineers generally need at least a bachelor's degree either in computer science or emphasizing programming and software development. Many employers want people with experience as well, and as with programmers, expanding the skill set with additional courses is important.

Despite recent difficulties in the industry, the job outlook is excellent. In fact, computer software engineering is expected to expand faster than any other occupation through 2010. Median annual earnings for applications engineers were about $68,000 in 2000; systems engineers could expect a little more. In 2001, new computer engineering bachelor's graduates received average starting offers of almost $54,000; new master's graduates averaged $58,000. In computer science, new bachelor's graduates averaged starting offers of almost $53,000. Software development engineers could start at $63,000 to $92,000.

SYSTEMS ANALYSIS AND DATABASE ADMINISTRATION

The nation's 887,000 systems analysts, computer scientists, and database administrators make up one of the fastest growing occupations, at least through 2010. *Systems analysts* analyze user needs and design hardware and software systems—including databases—to meet those needs. Their task begins with defining the nature of a data processing or calculation problem. They then break the problem into component parts; define necessary data, equipment, and processing steps; and instruct computer programmers in how to go about putting the problem "on the computer." They deal with a great variety of problems, from devising inventory systems and installing computers to forecasting sales and monitoring nuclear power plants. Some computer scientists and systems analysts do research to devise new and more powerful methods of systems analysis, design new computers, and develop new applications.

Programmer-analysts work specifically with software. *Network systems analysts* and *data communications analysts* work with networks. *Internet* or *web developers* (or *web designers*) design and operate websites, including those that handle the ever-growing amount of E-commerce activity. *Database administrators* design and maintain databases that store corporate and government data. Among their concerns are safeguarding data against loss and unauthorized access.

Systems analysts and database administrators generally need at least a bachelor's degree in computer science, information science, or management information systems (MIS), which includes courses related to accounting and business management. Many employers want to see a master's in business administration (M.B.A.) with plenty of course work in information or computer science. Some employers want the degree in a computer field, with less emphasis on the field of application. Many systems analysts have transferred from jobs as programmers. Graduate degrees are essential for the more complex jobs and for academic positions. Experience can lead to supervisory and management posts.

In 2000, computer systems analysts averaged about $60,000 per year. Database administrators could expect about $52,000. Network systems and data communication analysts averaged over $54,000. In 2001, new bachelor's graduates in computer systems analysis received average starting offers of $45,643. New MIS graduates could expect average salaries of almost $46,000.

COMPUTER SERVICE

Since computers are complex machines, they break down, and the computer industry depends heavily on computer repairers, or service technicians—172,000 of them in 2000. *Computer service technicians* diagnose and repair breakdowns in computers and their peripheral equipment (such as printers) as well as other office machines. They also perform routine maintenance—adjusting, cleaning, and oiling mechanical and electromechanical parts—and help install new equipment.

The demand for computer service technicians is high, but job growth is expected to be only average through 2010. Some work for large computer users, who can expect enough malfunctions to keep one or more technicians busy. Many work for computer makers or lessors, working out of central offices to serve many computer users. Their pay averaged $30,000 ($15 per hour) in 2000. Senior technicians with several years of experience may earn over $45,000 a year.

The basic education for a job as a computer service technician requires one or two years of post–high school education in electronics or electrical engineering, obtained from a vocational school, a community college, or a four-year college or university. The necessary training is also available in the military. Further training on the job lasts six months to two years. Certification programs are available through the Computing Technology Industry Association, the International Society of Certified Electronics Technicians, and the Electronics Technicians Association.

COMPUTER SUPPORT AND SYSTEMS ADMINISTRATION

Computer support and systems administration is another rapidly growing area. In 2000, there were 506,000 computer support specialists and 229,000 network and computer systems administrators. *Computer support specialists* provide technical support. They work both for software and hardware vendors and for MIS departments, where they operate help desks for corporate employees. Because an important part of their work is diagnosing problems, they must be up-to-date on the latest technologies. They must also be good at dealing with people. *Network* and *computer systems administrators* design, set up, and maintain internal organizational networks (LANs and intranets) and external networks (WANs and Internet segments). They deal with hardware, software, and security issues; some even specialize in security.

Most employers want at least some college education, preferably including computer courses. Lacking a college degree, certification is essential. As with programmers (see earlier), maintaining and expanding one's "skill set" with courses and programs is essential.

In 2000, computer support specialists averaged over $36,000. Network and computer systems administrators averaged about $51,000. In 2001, help-desk staff could expect to start at about $30,000. More senior technical support people could expect $48,000 to $61,000. Systems administrators could start at $50,000 to $70,000.

OPERATIONS RESEARCH

The nation's 47,000 *operations research analysts* (also known as *management scientists*) deal with scheduling, forecasting, resource allocation, product mix, and distribution, using the principles of mathematics and logic to define organizational problems, break the problems into manageable pieces, and seek efficient, effective solutions. Their tools are the mathematics of linear programming and game theory, computer simulations, and systems analysis. They work intimately with both computers and the people whose work centers on the problems at issue. This kind of quantitative analysis is crucial to corporate and government decision making, but employment of operations research analysts is expected to grow only slowly through 2010. The reason is that many people who do the same work bear other job titles, such as systems analyst, policy analyst, or operations analyst.

Operations research analysts must generally have a master's degree in the field or in engineering, mathematics, information systems, or computer science. Training continues on the job, for new workers are often paired with experienced hands. Their skills must be strong in the areas of database management, programming, and systems analysis. They must also have good "people" skills. Experienced analysts may move into management.

In 2000, operations research analysts averaged over $53,000. In 2001, federal operations research analysts averaged almost $78,000.

HOT SPOTS

The best job outlook among mathematicians is for accountants, but even this group faces nowhere near the prospects of computer workers. Programmers, software engineers, systems analysts, and database administrators all enjoy high pay and ample job opportunities, and the situation is bound to get even better.

The reason is simple: computers still represent an emerging technology. In the past fifty years, they have shrunk greatly in size and cost and grown tremendously in usefulness. Less than $1,000 will now buy more computing power than the founders of the field dreamed of, and it can fit in one hand rather than an entire air-conditioned building. And the technology is continuing to evolve.

At the same time, the falling costs and rising powers of computers mean that each generation finds more uses for the machines. In the last few years, E-commerce has come to play a major role in the economy. M-commerce (M for mobile) is the new watchword; it depends on the recent proliferation of PDAs (Personal Digital Assistants, such as the Palm computer), Internet-capable cell phones, and wireless networking. Automobiles and appliances now incorporate computers. Robots are reaching the market. And so on. There is no end in sight.

As a side effect, there is a huge demand for writing about computers. There are already many computer magazines and a host of books (including textbooks) for both experts and novices.

CAREERS ON CAMPUS

We have already noted that most pure mathematicians work as teachers and researchers at colleges and universities. Applied mathematicians usually find more lucrative employment in industry. The same goes for statisticians, actuaries, accountants, and computer people. There are, however, university and college positions in all of these fields, and each field advances at least in part by academic research. This is especially true for the computer sciences, as schools and departments of computer and information science are responsible for many of the latest improvements in computer science, including the fascinating progress that has been made in the field of artificial intelligence. Computer people, applied and pure mathematicians, and statisticians also find work in campus-affiliated and independent research centers. Many moonlight as consultants as well.

CAREERS IN INDUSTRY

Most mathematics and computer workers are employed by industry, for that is where the need for information processing is greatest. Researchers are concentrated on campus, but sometimes the best or only way to deal with topics at the frontiers of knowledge and to do so with adequate equipment is to work for the private sector. Microsoft and IBM, among other companies, sponsor a great deal of cutting-edge research.

CAREERS IN GOVERNMENT

Government needs actuaries, accountants, auditors, bookkeepers, computer scientists, computer operators, programmers, service technicians, systems and operations research analysts, mathematicians, and statisticians in every branch. Financial workers find jobs in the Internal Revenue Service, Treasury Department, and Office of Management and Budget, as well as on congressional staffs and in those parts of the Defense, Energy, Education, Interior, and other departments that deal with budgets. Mathematicians work for the Departments of Defense and Energy and to a lesser extent elsewhere. Computer scientists, systems analysts, and database, network, and security specialists play important roles in the Departments of Defense and Homeland Security, among others. Statisticians play vital roles in the Department of Commerce's National Bureau of Standards, Bureau of the Census, and Bureau of Economic Analysis; the Defense Department; the Department of Education's National Center for Education Statistics; the Department of Energy's Information Administration; the Department of Health and Human Services' National Center for Health Statistics and National Institutes of Health; the Department of Justice's Bureau of Justice Statistics; the Department of Labor's Bureau of Labor Statistics; and many other agencies. At lower levels, they process the data on which the government runs. At higher levels, they may actually help make government policy.

ORGANIZATIONS FOR MATHEMATICIANS AND COMPUTER SCIENTISTS

Most professional organizations for mathematicians and computer scientists offer career pamphlets for students and others contemplating the direction of their future lives. Many offer help in finding jobs. They may also offer lists of schools whose programs in their fields are approved or accredited. All hold periodic meetings at which members can exchange information, present papers, socialize, and seek jobs.

Societies and Sources of Further Information for Careers in Mathematics and Computer Science

American Academy of Actuaries
1100 17th Street, NW, 7th Floor
Washington, DC 20036
www.actuary.org/index.htm

American Institute of Certified Public Accountants
1211 Avenue of the Americas
New York, NY 10036-8775
www.aicpa.org

American Mathematical Society
201 Charles Street
Providence, RI 02940
www.ams.org

American Society of Pension Actuaries
4245 N. Fairfax Drive, Suite 750
Arlington, VA 22203
www.aspa.org

American Statistical Association
1429 Duke Street
Alexandria, VA 22314
www.amstat.org

Association for Computing Machinery
1515 Broadway
New York, NY 10036
www.acm.org

Association of Computer Support Specialists
218 Huntington Road
Bridgeport, CT 06608
www.acss.org

Casualty Actuarial Society
1100 N. Glebe Road, Suite 600
Arlington, VA 22201
www.beanactuary.org

Computing Technology Industry Association
450 E. 22nd Street, Suite 230
Lombard, IL 60148-6158
www.comptia.org

Electronics Technicians Association, International
5 Depot Street
Greencastle, IN 46135
www.eta-sda.com

IEEE Computer Society
1730 Massachusetts Avenue, NW
Washington, DC 20036-1992
www.computer.org

Institute for Certification of Computing Professionals
2350 E. Devon Avenue, Suite 115
Des Plaines, IL 60018
www.iccp.org

Institute for Operations Research and the Management Sciences
901 Elkridge Landing Road, Suite 400
Linthicum, MD 21090
www.informs.org

Institute of Internal Auditors
247 Maitland Avenue
Altamonte Springs, FL 32701-4201
www.theiia.org/iia/index.cfm

Institute of Management Accountants
10 Paragon Drive
Montvale, NJ 07645-1718
www.imanet.org

Institute of Mathematical Statistics
9650 Rockville Pike, Suite L2310
Bethesda, MD 20814-3998
www.imstat.org

International Society of Certified Electronics Technicians
3608 Pershing Avenue
Fort Worth, TX 76107
www.iscet.org

National Council of Teachers of Mathematics
1906 Association Drive
Reston, VA 22091-1502
www.nctm.org

Society for Industrial and Applied Mathematics
3600 University City Science Center
Philadelphia, PA 19104-2688
www.siam.org/index.htm

Society of Actuaries
475 N. Martingale Road, Suite 800
Schaumburg, IL 60173-2226
www.soa.org

System Administrators Guild
2560 9th Street, Suite 215
Berkeley, CA 94710
www.sage.org

CHAPTER 11

CAREERS IN AND AROUND GOVERNMENT

Government is the nation's single largest employer. In 1999, the federal government employed 2,799,000 civilians; state and local government employed 17,506,000. All levels of the government together employed 20,306,000 of this country's 140 million employed civilians, or 14.5 percent of the labor force.

A great many scientists and engineers work for the public sector. In 1998, government employed 692,800 of them, as shown in Table 11.1.

States and cities offer many of the same jobs as Uncle Sam, but they do not pay as well as the federal government. They also offer less generous fringe benefits, such as sick leave, educational aid, vacations, insurance, and retirement pay. The people who work for the more local levels of government are often people who wish to live in a particular part of the country and are willing to forego income and other benefits in favor of lifestyle.

No one should make the mistake of assuming that employment numbers for one year promise anything about coming years. This is as true of government employment as it is of any other industry. The determining factor is money, which is governed by the priorities of the day, whatever they are. We can glimpse how this works if we look once more at how government funding of scientific and technological research and development (R&D) has changed over the years (see Table 1.3 in Chapter 1). Much of this funding goes to pay R&D workers employed by the government. The United States

Table 11.1 Scientists, Engineers, and Technicians Employed by Government, 1998

OCCUPATION	TOTAL	GOVERNMENT
Scientists, engineers, and technicians	**5,808,700**	**692,800**
Scientists	**708,000**	**198,600**
Physical scientists	199,800	45,700
Life scientists	173,500	73,500
Mathematical scientists	14,000	4,100
Social scientists	320,700	75,300
Computer systems analysts, engineers, and scientists	1,530,500	124,200
Engineers	**1,461,800**	**166,100**
Civil engineers	195,000	63,600
Electrical/electronics engineers	357,000	32,100
Mechanical engineers	219,700	11,600
Engineering and science technicians	**1,350,600**	**151,700**
Electrical/electronics technicians	334,800	16,200
Engineering technicians	436,500	84,900
Drafters	283,200	9,800
Science technicians	227,400	28,600
Surveyors	**110,000**	**18,200**
Computer programmers	**647,800**	**34,000**

Source: U.S. Department of Labor, Bureau of Labor Statistics, *Occupational Outlook Handbook, 2002–2003* (Washington, DC: U.S. Department of Labor, Bureau of Labor Statistics, 2002) and *Occupational Outlook Quarterly* (Spring 2002).

as a whole—government, industry, and other sectors—spent a total of $264,622,000 on R&D in 2000. The federal government's share was less than a third of that total, used in roughly equal portions to fund the activities of government, industry, and university and college researchers.

The federal government is particularly committed to R&D in certain major areas. As shown in Table 11.2, the Department of Defense gets the lion's share of R&D funds, followed by the Department of Health and Human Services and the National Aeronautics and Space Administration. The new Department of Homeland Security will show up in future tallies, for there is strong interest in developing and deploying technological tools in the fight against terrorism. Nevertheless, it seems likely that the basic order of priorities will remain much the same.

Table 11.2 Federal Obligations for Research and Development in Current Dollars, 1999–2001

FEDERAL DEPARTMENT	1999	2000*	2001*
Total Obligations	**75,341**	**79,470**	**81,526**
Dept. of Defense	35,646	36,876	36,397
Dept. of Health and Human Services	15,915	18,140	19,235
National Aeronautics and Space Administration	9,526	9,568	9,602
Dept. of Energy	6,010	6,306	6,793
National Science Foundation	2,506	2,656	3,180
Dept. of Agriculture	1,614	1,752	1,779
Dept. of Commerce	990	1,041	1,127

*Preliminary

Source: U.S. Department of Labor, Bureau of Labor Statistics, *Occupational Outlook Handbook, 2002–2003* (Washington, DC: U.S. Department of Labor, Bureau of Labor Statistics, 2002) and *Occupational Outlook Quarterly* (Spring 2002).

FEDERAL EMPLOYMENT SYSTEM

We have discussed federal employment in specific fields of science as we proceeded through this book. Now let us consider the way the federal employment system works.

The federal government fills some of its positions through contacts and journal and newspaper ads (see Chapter 12). Most often, however, it relies on the U.S. Office of Personnel Management (OPM; www.opm.gov). The OPM maintains the USAJOBS website (www.usajobs.opm.gov), which provides Internet-based access to job listings in many areas of government, as well as a mechanism for applying; for instance, for jobs with the Department of Agriculture, see www.usajobs.opm.gov/a9ag.htm.

According to the OPM, current procedures are much like those in private industry. Applicants may now contact government agencies directly for job information and application processing:

Previously the OPM maintained large standing registers of eligibles and required applicants to take standardized written tests. In addition, applicants completed a standard application form, the SF-171, to apply for all jobs. Today OPM no longer maintains registers of eligibles and only a few positions require a written test. The SF-171 is obsolete and no longer accepted by most Federal agencies. The new Federal application form is the

Optional Application for Federal Employment, OF-612. In lieu of submitting an OF-612, applicants may submit a résumé. Another change is that job seekers do not need a rating from OPM to enable them to apply for nonclerical vacancies. But, while the process is now very similar to that in private industry, there are still significant differences due to the many laws, executive orders, and regulations that govern federal employment.

Some "excepted" service agencies set their own qualification requirements and are not subject to the appointment, pay, and classification rules of the civil service.

The Postal Service (www.usps.com/employment), FBI (www.fbijobs .com), and CIA (www.cia.gov/cia/employment/ciaeindex.htm) have their own web-based systems. The Department of Commerce maintains the FedWorld site (www.fedworld.gov/jobs/jobsearch.html). Most states have similar systems.

GS GRADE SYSTEM

Federal government jobs have GS (General Schedule) or other (FO, EX, SES, SL, ST, and so on) "grades" according to their difficulty and level of responsibility; see Table 11.3 for pay ranges. The GS grading system applies to non-supervisory positions at all grade levels and for supervisory positions below grade 13. The designation GM is used for supervisory and management positions at GS grades 13, 14, and 15. The highest-level positions—supervisory personnel, such as agency directors, with grades above GS-15—are included in the Senior Executive Service, outside the General Schedule.

The grades are defined according to a position's knowledge requirement, need for supervision, complexity, reliance on rules or guidelines, and scope (among other things). The single most significant factor in assigning a GS grade to a job or employee is the knowledge requirement, or the education and training needed by the employee. The lowest GS grades require only knowledge of simple, routine, or repetitive tasks or operations that require little or no previous training or experience. Higher grades require a bachelor's degree. The highest grades require mastery of a professional field to the point where one can generate and develop new hypotheses and theories (the equivalent of a doctorate). Those who can handle complexity, exercise

Table 11.3 Pay Ranges for
General Schedule Jobs, 2002

GS LEVEL	PAY RANGE		
1	$14,757	to	$18,456
2	16,592	to	20,876
3	18,103	to	23,530
4	20,322	to	26,415
5	22,737	to	29,559
6	25,344	to	32,949
7	28,164	to	36,615
8	31,191	to	40,551
9	34,451	to	44,783
10	37,939	to	49,324
11	41,684	to	54,185
12	49,959	to	64,944
13	59,409	to	77,229
14	70,205	to	91,265
15	82,580	to	107,357

Source: U.S. Office of Personnel Management,
www.opm.gov

judgment and ingenuity, and work independently can earn higher grades. To reach the top of the GS ladder therefore requires both education and ability. For new employees who are just out of school, ability may be assessed by grade-point average, class ranking, or membership in national honorary societies, such as Phi Beta Kappa. Summer and part-time work experience also counts. As one progresses through one's career, experience may become the most important factor; the highest grades go to those with the most experience and the best track records. Senior Executive Service (SES) pay ranges from $121,600 to $166,700. Base pay for senior-level (SL) and scientific or professional (ST) positions ranges from $99,000 to $130,000.

Federal employment has several advantages. One is the pay. Another is that under the protection of the civil service system, job security is good and there is ample opportunity for advancement. A third advantage is that government employees may continue to receive full-time pay while continuing their education part-time (or full-time for up to one year). When they have finished the additional schooling, they are qualified for jobs at higher grade levels.

However, government biologists and other scientists have been fired or given unsatisfactory assignments for revealing errors or publicly disagreeing with their supervisors, who may be committed to a particular stance on a controversial issue such as nuclear energy, abortion, or environmental protection regulation. (Legal protection for "whistle-blowers" exists, but it is not always effective.) Also, government employees are restrained from political activity; they cannot help in political campaigns, and they must quit their jobs to run for office themselves.

CONGRESSIONAL FELLOWS

Congress deals constantly with issues of science and technology, and most senators and representatives have on staff people with scientific training and knowledge. These staff members may find their jobs through normal channels or by knowing a member of Congress and helping out in campaigns or as an unpaid science adviser. Young Ph.D.s may enter the congressional system through the Congressional Fellows Program (www .fellowships.aaas.org/overview.shtml), run by the American Association for the Advancement of Science (AAAS). The fellows are sponsored for one year by individual scientific societies, such as the AAAS itself, the American Society for Microbiology, the Biophysical Society, and the Federation of American Societies for Experimental Biology (FASEB) (nonbiological societies also take part in the program).

The program began in 1973 with seven fellows. Since then, it has expanded to sponsor dozens of fellows in nine fellowship programs: the Congressional Fellowship Program itself; the Roger Revelle Fellowship in Global Stewardship; the AAAS/NTI Fellowship in Global Security Program; the Diplomacy Fellowship Program; the Risk Policy Fellowship Program in Health, Safety and the Environment; the Defense Policy Fellowship Program; the Environmental Fellowship Program; the AAAS/NSF Science and Engineering Fellowship Program; and the AAAS/NIH Science Policy Fellowship Program.

The non-Congressional fellows occupy positions in the Department of State, the U.S. Agency for International Development, the Department of Agriculture, the Food and Drug Administration, the National Institutes of Health, the National Science Foundation, the Defense Department, and the Environmental Protection Agency and may go abroad as part of their service. Fellows are paid $58,000 per year; some positions may earn as much as $74,000. All the fellows are selected on the basis of excellence and interest in scientific and public policy. The program's aim, in the words of the AAAS, is "to provide the opportunity for accomplished and societally aware post-doctoral to midcareer scientists and engineers to participate in and contribute to the public policy making process of the federal government."

Congressional fellows begin their service with an intensive two-week orientation to government operations, focusing on issues involving science and public policy. For the next year, they work in Congress and various government agencies while participating in a year-long seminar on public policy. Past fellows have worked on legislation concerning health policy, environmental regulation, and energy. After a year in Washington, they generally return to campus or industry, but some remain in Washington. They may continue their work for Congress, enter other areas of government service, or even move toward high positions as heads of government agencies.

LOBBYISTS

It is also possible to work in Washington, D.C., or in state capitals without being on a government payroll at all. Most companies and industries—including universities, scientific societies, and professional groups, such as the American Medical Association—are vitally interested in government actions—in legislation, regulation, and policy formation. Naturally, they wish to influence these actions as much in their favor as they can. They thus provide information and opinion to legislators and bureaucrats. They cajole and persuade—they lobby—and their representatives, whether individuals or firms, are lobbyists.

The best lobbyists have some degree of sophistication in their particular area. Lobbyists on biological issues, for instance, may be practicing researchers or physicians, lobbying part-time on their own or as representatives of their employers. They may also be biologists who have left their fields to lobby full-time. They are all salespeople, and their function is exactly that of the sales force of a business: to explain technical matters clearly and to persuade the "customer" that their business deserves consideration and support.

Effective lobbyists are worth their weight in gold to industry. They can prevent a product ban, get a new product approved for sale, or reduce the need to spend money on pollution control or safety equipment. Their actions can result in millions of dollars for their employers, and they can be paid extremely well.

12

FINDING
JOBS

As I hope this book has made abundantly clear, there are a great many different possible careers in science. They require various levels of education and offer various degrees of pay. Some offer great room for advancement; some do not. Most offer recognition and the sense of self-worth that comes from knowing that one is doing useful, challenging work.

Many scientists find that the greatest advantage of their work is the feeling that they are not performing "just another job." Unlike workers in many other areas, they do not have to wait for weekends, vacations, and retirement to do what they really enjoy. They are already doing what they enjoy most, and they are getting paid for it.

Many people find that a career in science is more than a career. It is a way of life that provides the scientist's most valued pleasures, achievements, and gratifications. It is thus, perhaps, what any career should be, but too few are—demanding, absorbing, and fulfilling. Teachers are committed to educating young people, both in and out of the classroom. Researchers and technicians are constantly thinking of problems and solutions. Their work, like other people's hobbies, even enters their dinner-table and party conversations. The scientist's work is never far from his or her mind; a scientist never willingly drops it. Scientists need never find their work boring, unless they are in the wrong field, and they don't retire easily.

It is possible for a scientist to do research and teach informally without an actual scientific job. Once upon a time, in fact, this was how scientists survived. They were theologians, monks, philosophers, cloth merchants, and bureaucrats who pursued their science on the side, as a hobby. They were "amateurs," lovers of their field, unpaid except in satisfaction and—sometimes—fame. They accomplished wonders, and they laid the foundations of modern science.

But a job enables a scientist to do more. It allows more time for the field one loves. It often carries with it better equipment and facilities, easier access to colleagues, and a greater variety of rewards. And fortunately, science today is a professional activity, not a hobby. The scientist is expected to work as a scientist.

So how do scientists and others who wish to work in and around science find suitable jobs? How do they locate their professional niche? They choose their field. They obtain all the training needed. Now, how do they find that first job—an entry position?

At the lowest levels, this question has a simple answer. High school graduates find jobs as bookkeepers, for instance, by answering ads in newspapers. So can technicians, teachers, and researchers, but for them there are more fruitful avenues as well. The best of these avenues may be the one that starts with "contacts." Everyone can use it, from high school grads to Ph.D.s.

However, before we go into detail about contacts and other job sources, we need to say a few words about something every job seeker needs: a résumé.

RÉSUMÉS

At heart a résumé is a very simple document. It lists one's education, special skills, and experience in a format that permits a potential employer—who may be sorting through hundreds of applications for a single job—to extract the gist quickly and efficiently. For a person fresh out of school, the résumé's chief content will be the degree obtained, languages (foreign and computer programming) studied, special accomplishments, and honors or awards earned. Part-time and summer jobs should be listed as well, for they do say something about one's attitude toward work.

Common advice holds that one should limit the length of a résumé to one page. This is easily done for a new graduate. For someone who has been out of school for a few years, however, it may not be possible. The more experience one has, the more space the list of jobs, projects, tasks, responsibilities, and accomplishments will take up. And if one has publications and/or patents to cite, the résumé will grow even longer.

The best advice is surely to put the most important elements of one's résumé —education, training, and special skills—on the first page. After that, the prescription varies according to one's individual history and field. There are a great many books available on how to put together an effective résumé; several of these are designed for those seeking careers in the sciences.

CONTACTS

Earlier in this book we stressed that college and graduate students can gain valuable experience and pay some of their educational bills by working part-time and summers as research or teaching assistants. They may work for a faculty member at their school or at a nearby lab, museum, or other institution. They may find work by asking one of their professors or by replying to an on-campus announcement. College and university departments and school financial aid or placement offices may post lists of available part-time and summer positions.

Finding work this way depends on being in the right place, close to the right people, at the right time. This is the essence of the "contact"—someone who knows the job seeker and whom the job seeker can reach easily. And contacts can be a great help later, too. As students near graduation, many of them find that their department, their faculty adviser, or the professors they work for know of fellowships, postdoctoral positions, and teaching and research jobs in the academic world, in government, and in industry. That knowledge may come from flyers mailed out by employers looking for new graduates or from colleagues elsewhere who have asked, "Do you know someone good for this job?" A recommendation from a professor whom an employer knows and trusts may be the best possible credential for a job.

Students can find it a great help to attend scientific meetings in their field whenever possible. On these occasions, they will meet many people and establish their own contacts. They will find that many of the people they meet have their ears open for job opportunities, while others are looking for potential employees. The main purpose of scientific meetings is supposedly the exchange of scientific information, but it is sometimes said that job hunting gets just as much, or more, attention.

Are contacts useful only at the beginning of a working career? Not at all. They may very well help match the student with a first job, but then the student begins to establish a reputation as a teacher, researcher, technician, administrator, or whatever. The worker becomes known to others in the field and finds that prospective employers approach him or her at meetings or by phone or mail. Perhaps the employer is drawn by the worker's reputation or was given the worker's name by a former professor or a mutual friend. Perhaps they were coworkers at another job, or perhaps they met at a convention. In all such cases, the potential job comes because of contacts that the worker has made in the past.

Jobs found through contacts may be the best ones. They usually mean that someone who knows both the job and the worker believes that the two belong together, and that someone is often right. Jobs found through other means may be less likely to fit the worker perfectly.

It is thus a good idea to cultivate as many contacts as possible. Students should work with their professors. Students and graduates should attend meetings, meet people, and join research, engineering, design, and other kinds of teams. They should never work alone if they can avoid it, for that insulates them from contacts and may limit their future choice of jobs.

CAMPUS PLACEMENT OFFICES

Many two- and four-year colleges and graduate schools have placement or career services offices. They may list mainly on-campus jobs open to students. They may also list off-campus jobs that are open to present students and recent graduates. In the latter case, the placement office is more useful to the new worker seeking a career position in industry or on another campus.

Placement offices also help students prepare their résumés, among other things (see the boxed feature on page 203 for a list of the services offered at one college). This is a straightforward enough task, and there are many available sources on how to do it, from "professional writing" text-

---

Career Services at Thomas College

The Career Services office at Thomas College in Waterville, Maine, offers Thomas students the following services:

- Career advising, counseling, and self-assessment opportunities
- Help developing résumés and cover letters that work
- Employment search strategies
- Interview preparation
- Workshops
- On-campus recruiting
- Career Information Days
- Internship guidance and support
- Online job and internship postings
- Part-time and summer work listings
- Networking opportunities with area employers and alumni
- Job shadows
- Maintaining student credential files

---

books to job-hunting manuals. However, it is also a task that baffles many young job seekers, and the help in preparing résumés that campus placement offices offer prompts many students to bless them.

Finally, placement offices—especially those at larger schools—often arrange for prospective employers in industry and government to send "recruiters" to campus. They set a date for, say, Campus Career Days. The recruiters arrive together, and they may all have booths or tables in one location, such as the school gym. They then interview interested students who are near graduation. When they find students whose backgrounds, education, talents, and interests match vacant niches in their organizations, they may invite these students to visit their headquarters for further interviews. They may, on occasion, make actual job offers on the spot, and fortunate students in high-demand fields may have their pick of thirty or more job offers.

INQUIRIES

Getting a job, whether through contacts, through placement offices, or by answering ads, requires an initial approach. It may be face-to-face at a professional meeting, by phone, or—most often—by mail. Job seekers generally write letters of inquiry. These letters describe the job seeker and his or her background, say what job the seeker wants as specifically as possible, and say what good the job seeker can do the employer.

If a colleague, a professor, or a friend has suggested contacting the employer, the letter should say so. It should be addressed to some specific person at the employer's office, and it should make clear that the job seeker knows something about the employer's operations and has some idea of how he or she might fit in. Today, it is very easy to find out at least basic information about any organization you wish to investigate. Use the Internet! Type the name of the organization into a search engine such as Google. If you know the names of people associated with the organization, type in those, too (but be careful—there can be more than one person with the same name, and it is not always wise to mention everything you find out this way).

For example, Janine Latrobe is a geophysical consultant working out of Detroit. Peter Jeffers, a friend who works as a geologist for GeoSystems, Inc., in Tucson, writes to say that his firm has just accepted a contract to build a geothermal energy plant. He remembers that Janine has been involved with similar projects in the past. Would she be interested in coming to Tucson? They will be needing a head for the design team. The chief of the engineering department is Iosip Wilkov.

Janine is interested. She Googles GeoSystems, Inc., and learns that the company doesn't just have one new contract. According to industry reports, it is aggressively marketing affordable, efficient geothermal energy systems, and utility companies are expressing a great deal of interest. It thus looks like the company could be a very good bet for a long-term position. She then Googles Iosip Wilkov and learns that he got his master's degree from the same university she went to (although not at the same time). She now writes directly to Iosip Wilkov, not to the personnel department. She says something along these lines:

> *Peter Jeffers, a GeoSystems geologist, recently wrote me that you*
> *will soon begin work on a geothermal energy plant and may need*
> *a geophysicist to lead your design team.*
>
> *As a geophysical consultant for the last nine years, I have worked*
> *with some very challenging geothermal projects. In one, the problem*

was high-pressure fluids. In another, it was very corrosive fluids. In both cases, I helped find the solution. You can call [names, phone numbers, company names] if you have any questions about my competence.

Mr. Jeffers did not tell me a great deal about your particular geothermal energy project, but I know that you have promising technology and exciting prospects ahead. I am confident that I can help, and I would love to be involved.

I look forward to talking with you to learn the details and to filling out a formal application for the job.

She then says when she can come to Tucson, describes the current projects she is working on, and encloses her résumé and letters of recommendation. She is confident—as she should be—that her letter will be far more effective than one that fails to relate her to both the employer and the job. The only thing she might have done differently is to call Iosip Wilkov first to learn some of the details of the job and confirm that there is indeed an opening. In her letter, she could then have related herself to the details. She could also have begun her letter with a more personal touch: "As we discussed on the phone yesterday. . . ." She could even have mentioned the university background that she and Mr. Wilkov share, though perhaps it is better to save that for conversation after they meet or even to let him notice it once he sees her résumé.

Answering job ads is a little more difficult. The ads often spend a paragraph describing the job, but they don't reveal a great deal of detail. Again, a phone call can help. If you have a friend who works for the advertising employer, calling that friend can reveal details, such as specific projects or goals that the "contact name" in the ad might not even know. Such details can help you write a very convincing letter.

PROFESSIONAL SOCIETIES

Like colleges and universities, professional societies often provide job information. Many publish journals that list job openings. The American Association for the Advancement of Science (AAAS) publishes *Science*, whose ads cover the gamut of disciplines and employers—academic, industrial, and government. The AAAS website (www.aaas.org/careers) also offers a wealth of resources for job seekers, including ads, salary surveys, and more.

Many professional societies, with their web addresses, are listed at the ends of previous chapters. Most offer career and job information tailored to the particular discipline. For instance, the American Chemical Society (www.chemistry.org) offers a great many career resources, including notices of national and regional meetings where job seekers and employers can meet for interviews. It also offers résumé assistance, career consultation, interview practice, and job ads. The Association for Computing Machinery (ACM) offers a little less at www.jobcentre.acm.org/search.cfm.

JOB ADS

Besides the ads in professional journals and on professional society websites, there are also ads in publications that focus on particular industries. The *Chronicle of Higher Education* concentrates on academic posts and publishes a great many ads each week, both on paper and on their website (www.chronicle.com/jobs). HigherEdJobs (www.higheredjobs.com) posts similar jobs online only; it permits job seekers to search job listings, post résumés for potential employers to see, and even be informed via E-mail when jobs matching their goals are advertised.

Anyone looking for a job through ads should not neglect the larger newspapers and the weekend editions of smaller ones. They advertise a wealth of positions on campus, in industry, and in government—in all fields and at all levels. The difference is that many of their ads are for jobs in the newspaper's city, state, or region, which can prove very useful to the job seeker who wants to settle or remain in a particular locale.

USING THE INTERNET

The Internet is an invaluable resource for anyone looking for a job. There are sites for professional societies and industries and also sites for specific fields. Anyone interested in careers related to the environment should be aware of the Environmental Jobs and Careers site (www.ecoemploy.com) and the Environmental Career Center (www.environmentalcareer.com).

More general sites include Monster.com (www.monster.com), which permits job seekers to search job listings, post résumés for potential employers to see, and even be informed via e-mail when jobs matching their goals are advertised. Online services such as Yahoo offer a similar array of services (see www.hotjobs.yahoo.com).

For government jobs, the U.S. Office of Personnel Management (OPM; opm.gov) maintains the USAJOBS website (www.usajobs.opm.gov), which provides access to job listings in many areas of government, as well as a mechanism for applying.

The U.S. Department of Labor runs America's Job Bank (www.ajb .dni.us), which calls itself "the biggest and busiest job market in cyberspace. Job seekers can post their résumé where thousands of employers search every day, search for job openings automatically, and find their dream job fast. Employers can post job listings in the nation's largest online labor exchange, create customized job orders, and search résumés automatically to find the right people fast."

There are also guides to Internet job searching. One very complete, user-friendly guide is *The Guide to Internet Job Searching, 2004–2005*, by Margaret Riley Dikel, Frances E. Roehm, and the Public Library Association (VGM Career Books, a division of the McGraw-Hill Companies, 2004).

BIBLIOGRAPHY

AAAS Report XXVIII: Research and Development Fiscal Year 2004. March 31, 2003. aaas.org/spp/rd/fy04.htm.

Committee on Science, Engineering, and Public Policy. *Enhancing the Post-doctoral Experience for Scientists and Engineers: A Guide for Postdoctoral Scholars, Advisers, Institutions, Funding Organizations, and Disciplinary Societies.* Washington, DC: National Academy Press, 2000.

Committee on Science, Engineering, and Public Policy. *On Being a Scientist: Responsible Conduct in Research.* 2nd ed. Washington, DC: National Academy Press, 1995.

Denning, Peter, J. "Career Redux." *Communications of the ACM* 45, 9 (September 2002): 21–26.

Dreyfus, Hubert. *What Machines Still Can't Do.* Cambridge, MA: MIT Press, 1992.

Easton, Thomas A., ed. *Taking Sides: Clashing Views on Controversial Issues in Science, Technology and Society.* 6th ed. Guilford, CT: McGraw-Hill/ Dushkin, 2004.

Flores, Fernando, and John Gray. *Entrepreneurship and the Wired Life: Work in the Wake of Careers.* London: Demos, 2000.

Fountain, Melvin. "Matching Yourself with the World of Work." *Occupational Outlook Quarterly,* Fall 1986.

Holland, J. L. *Making Vocational Choices: A Theory of Vocational Personalities and Work Environments.* 3rd ed. Lutz, FL: Psychological Assessment Resources, 1997.

Holland, J. L. *The Self-Directed Search*. Palo Alto, CA: Consulting Psychologists Press, 1977.

Holland, J. L. *Understanding Yourself and Your Career*. Palo Alto, CA: Consulting Psychologists Press, 1977.

Jaffe, Sam, and Paula Park. "Postdocs: Pawing Out of Purgatory." *The Scientist* 17, 6 (March 24, 2003): 46–48.

Medawar, P. B. *Advice to a Young Scientist*. New York: Harper & Row, 1979.

Mullin, James. "Changing Patterns of Research Funding (1960–2000)." *International Social Science Journal* 53, 168 (June 2001). 247–270.

National Science Board. *Science and Engineering Indicators, 2002*. Arlington, VA: National Science Foundation, 2002. NSB-02-1.

Reardon, Robert C., and Janet G. Lenz. *Self-Directed Search and Related Holland Career Materials: A Practitioner's Guide*. Lutz, FL: Psychological Assessment Resources, 1998.

Renner, Michael. *Working for the Environment: A Growing Source of Jobs*. Washington, DC: Worldwatch Institute, 2000.

U.S. Department of Commerce, U.S. Census Bureau, *Statistical Abstract of the United States 2001*. Washington, D.C.: U.S. Census Bureau, 2002.

U.S. Department of Labor, Bureau of Labor Statistics. *Occupational Outlook Handbook, 2002–03*. Chicago, IL: VGM Career Books, 2002.

Whitehead, Jr., Ralph, and Robert J. Lacey. "College and Knowledge: A New View of the State's Labor Force." *Massachusetts Economic Benchmarks* 5, 3 (Summer 2002): www.massbenchmarks.org. 12–15.

ABOUT
THE AUTHOR

Professor of Science Thomas A. Easton holds a doctorate in theoretical biology from the University of Chicago and teaches at Thomas College in Waterville, Maine. His books *Taking Sides: Clashing Views on Controversial Issues in Science, Technology and Society* (6th ed., 2004) and *Taking Sides: Clashing Views on Controversial Environmental Issues* (10th ed., 2003) are available from McGraw-Hill/Dushkin.

Dr. Easton is also a well-known science fiction critic, with a monthly book-review column in the science fiction magazine *Analog*, and a member of the Science Fiction and Fantasy Writers of America. His latest novels are *The Great Flying Saucer Conspiracy* (Wildside, 2002) and *Firefight* (Betancourt and Company, 2003).